LIFE ON THE ROCKS

LIFE ON THE

BRUCE L. SMITH

ROCKS

A Portrait of the American Mountain Goat

University Press of Colorado

© 2014 by Bruce L. Smith

Published by University Press of Colorado
5589 Arapahoe Avenue, Suite 206C
Boulder, Colorado 80303

 The University Press of Colorado is a proud member of
the Association of American University Presses.

The University Press of Colorado is a cooperative publishing enterprise supported, in part, by Adams State University, Colorado State University, Fort Lewis College, Metropolitan State University of Denver, Regis University, University of Colorado, University of Northern Colorado, Utah State University, and Western State Colorado University.

∞ The paper used in this publication meets the minimum requirements of the American National Standard for Information Sciences—Permanence of Paper for Printed Library Materials. ANSI Z39.48-1992

Library of Congress Cataloging-in-Publication Data

Smith, Bruce L., 1948–
 Life on the rocks : a portrait of the American mountain goat / by Bruce L. Smith, Ph.D.
    pages cm
 Includes bibliographical references.
 ISBN 978-1-60732-291-7 (cloth) — ISBN 978-1-60732-292-4 (ebook)
 1. Mountain goat. I. Title.
 QL737.U53S63 2014
 599.64′75—dc23

                                        2013036242

Design by Daniel Pratt

23 22 21 20 19 18 17 16 15 14   10 9 8 7 6 5 4 3 2 1

Cover photographs by Bruce L. Smith

Contents

It's a long way down.
(Photo by author)

Far above where most humans venture, where the upthrust peaks embrace the heavens, a gentleman dressed in a shaggy white cloak roams the heights. Trimmed in beard, baggy pants, black nose, and stiletto horns, he rambles the ridgetops amid blinding snow and biting wind, where winter reigns half of the year. Perhaps the most extraordinary mountaineer to ever live, this Old Man of the Mountains is America's mountain goat.

I became interested in mountain goats as a student studying wildlife biology at the University of Montana. That state's mule deer, elk, pronghorn, moose, and bighorn sheep were a beguiling assemblage of ungulates (hoofed animals) to this Michigan transplant. In 1971, during a Thanksgiving weekend visit to the home of my college roommate's parents in Great Falls, I first made acquaintance with the mountain goat. Beholding an unblinking head that austerely poked from the wall, I thought this was the most elegant beast that I had ever seen.

Twenty miles south of Missoula, Montana, and beyond sprawled the nearest population's retreat where I spent future weekends searching for the real thing. My fascination grew with each sighting of these wind-racked apparitions, clinging to the ragged edge of the Selway-Bitterroot Wilderness Area—at that time, the largest designated wilderness in the lower forty-eight states. Following a senior thesis of finding and counting them in winter, I fashioned a research proposal for a graduate degree program. From 1973 to 1975, I tromped the glacially carved canyons that spilled eastward from the crests of the Bitterroot Mountains to the river below. Focused on the environmental bottleneck that most tests the goats, I spent three winters and springs studying and marveling at their adaptations and behaviors so suited to life among the peaks. Throughout a conservation career in which large mammals dominated my field studies, again and again I returned to goat ranges in the United States and Canada to witness their high wire acts.

Wildlife photography, much like scientific research, is often a solitary pursuit. Stalking the animals with enough sensitivity to not alarm them—or, better yet, positioning oneself so the animals find the viewfinder on their own—takes the kind of patience that only the mountain goat may truly own. Capturing their images should not be rushed, in part because gravity happens quickly. One fall that broke a bone and another swift trip I took down a slope in an avalanche were reminders of the perils that the goats face daily.

Most of the photographs I've chosen for this book are from those frigid months when goats confront nature's rigors with tenacity and grace. Gripping the grim limits of possibility, this is among the continent's most remarkable of inhabitants—a testament to nature's abhorrence of a biotic vacuum. Yet, despite the apparent security of its wilderness realm, America's mountain goat faces mounting challenges in a changing world. For no species lives far or deep or lofty enough to escape the pervasive reach of humankind—not the polar bear, the whale, or the eagle, not even the mountain goat.

By sharing these images, words, and my affection for the animal, my hope is to bring greater appreciation and attention to the conservation needs of this American athlete of the alpine.

Intense light, snow, and gravity—extreme elements of the mountain goat's lofty domain—make the bearded beast a challenging subject to photograph. (Photo by author)

LIFE ON THE ROCKS

Like a ghost that drifts among clouds and cliffs, in defiance of gravity itself, abides this improbable beast of the peaks. From the loftiest vantage of any large mammal on the continent, it has watched the comings and goings of others over untold generations. This time-tested perspective accords the Old Man of the Mountains some authority on success and failure and what conditions render each. We may do well to take heed.

Part I

DOI: 10.5876_9781607322924.c001

From American Indians, the Corps of Discovery first heard about a white beast that dwelt among the peaks. They marveled at the shaggy hide purchased from Chinookan Indians along the Columbia River. In 1805 Captain William Clark even glimpsed a live one, albeit at a great distance, near what now is the Idaho-Montana border.

In 1778 Captain James Cook recorded the earliest hint of the creature's existence. During stops at British Columbia and Alaskan villages on his around-the-world voyage, he was struck by the spun wool garments worn by the natives. When the Indians pointed out white animals perched high on the rocks as the source of the garments' wool, Cook called them polar bears.

Others have confused the animal with mountain sheep, which also occupy the continent's western mountains. Indeed the English translation of the mountain goat's taxonomic genus, *Oreamnos*, suggests as much—lamb of the mountains.

Still others reckoned the beast bearing a shoulder hump and simple black horns as a new variety of a familiar species. In 1798, Alexander McKenzie described the animal he spotted in the mountains near the McKenzie River as a white buffalo. Although albino bison do exist, McKenzie's arctic animal was likely the mountain goat.

Just as fascinating and incomparable as the mountain goat are the topography and geology of the realm the animal inhabits. (Photo by author)

Curious yet cautious, a goat peers over a lichen-encrusted rock. (Photo by author)

From Alaska's Kenai Fiords to Washington's Mount Shuksan (this photo), ice, rock, and stunning scenery typify the domain of the mountain goat. (Photo by author)

It's not hard to imagine how the early explorers, trappers, and fortune-seekers might find the notion of a white buffalo roaming the mountaintops as much reality as phantom or fable. Some 25–50 million bison once roamed the continent and were well known to most who ventured west. Even in fiction, the taxonomy of this stout-shouldered creature was enigmatic. A passage from *The Big Sky*, Pulitzer prize-winning author A. B. Guthrie's yarn about the mountain men of Montana, describes the mountain goat this way:

> It ain't a buffler proper, nor a white antelope, neither, though you hear the name put
> to it and a sight of others. They keep to the high peaks, they do, the tip top of moun-
> tains, in the clouds and snow. . . . Not many's seen a live one. A man has to climb
> some for that.

Native people of North America's First Nations, of course, had known the animal for centuries. Some hunted them for food, ceremonial items, and clothing. But well into the twentieth century, these wilderness cliff-walkers were relatively untouched by the westward march of Euro-Americans. It was an animal more of myth and mystery than avarice, and thus it escaped the tsunami of exploitation suffered by the more easily targeted bison, pronghorn, deer, elk, and the goat's mountain cousin the bighorn sheep.

Along with its closest relatives that inhabit European and Asian peaks, the mountain goat completes a distinct taxonomic grouping, the Rupicaprini Tribe (*Rupes* = rock, *capra* = goat), within the sheep, goat, antelope, and cattle family (the Bovidae). The rupicaprids are regarded as goat-antelopes, possessing traits of both true goats and antelopes but are neither. Characteristic of the mountain goat and its relations—and distinguishing those species from other members of the Bovidae family—are their thin-boned and fragile skulls, and short, dagger-like horns that look similar in both sexes.

The mountain goat's rupicaprid relatives are the mysterious gorals and serows of Asia, and the chamois of Europe. The total number of species depends upon which taxonomist you ask, but there may be as many as four species of goral and between three and six species of serows (see *Walker's Mammals of the World* and *Mammal Species of the World* for species accounts). Most authorities agree on two species of chamois—*Rupicapra pyrenaica* of the Pyrenees and Apennine Mountains of France, Spain, and Italy, and the more abundant *Rupicapra rupicapra* of the Alps, the Balkans, Asia Minor, and the Caucasus.

The gorals (all of the genus *Naemorhedus*) are the most primitive rupicaprids and likely the most similar in appearance to the ancestral form that gave rise to the modern tribal descendants. The gorals are grayish or reddish, coarse-haired, short-horned, and most weigh fifty to seventy-five pounds as adults. The species' geographic range includes mountainous regions of eastern Russia and China, Thailand, Myanmar, Vietnam, and possibly Laos. A population of the species called the long-tailed goral occupies the demilitarized zone of the Korean Peninsula.

An adult Chinese goral (*Naemorhedus griseus*) (Photo by author)

An adult Japanese serow (*Capricornis crispus*) (Photo by author)

An adult European chamois (*Rupicapra rupicapra*) (Courtesy Valentina Ruco)

An adult musk ox (*Ovibos moschatus*) (Photo by author)

Also resident to Asian mountains and ranging from Siberia south across the Himalayan region through Myanmar and Thailand to Malaya and Sumatra are the serows, all of the genus *Capricornis*. Resembling robust versions of gorals, they weigh up to 200 pounds and are reddish brown to gray-brown in color. Leading even more secretive lives than the gorals, the serows inhabit steep hillsides cloaked in dense vegetation. Isolated when the Japanese archipelago broke from the Asian mainland, the Japanese serow is perhaps the best known of the serows and gorals, which are among the least studied of the world's large mammals. Historic ranges of gorals and serows have been reduced by excessive hunting and habitat loss. Several species are now considered in danger of extinction.

The chamois, on the other hand, is the best known and studied among this small group of mountain dwellers. Easily the fleetest of the bunch and a prodigious leaper, the chamois is longer-legged and slimmer than other rupicaprids. Adults weigh seventy-five to one hundred pounds, are tawny to reddish brown in color with distinctive white markings, and are more gregarious than the gorals and serows of Asia.

The rupicaprids likely evolved in the Himalayan Plateau region and are considered to be more primitive than—seeming living ancestors of—the true goats and sheep. Their origins date back to the late Miocene Epoch and the tribe diversified into many species during the Pleistocene (0.1–1.8 million years ago), though most did not outlive the ice ages.

From the most northerly distribution of the modern-day serow and goral, the ancestral mountain goat crossed to the New World via the Bering Land Bridge during the Pleistocene—perhaps 40,000 or more years ago, when ocean levels were 300 feet lower than today. Molecular studies suggest a closer relationship between the mountain goat and another immigrant, the musk ox (*Ovibos moschatus*), than other North American large mammals. Yet America's goat-antelope resembles no other beast of either the New or Old World. It's an evolutionary novelty, one of a kind.

In short, the mountain goat is a mountain-dwelling ruminant, physically adapted for rock climbing and surviving arctic alpine weather. Although commonly called the Rocky Mountain goat, I prefer American mountain goat (or just mountain goat) because *Oreamnos americanus* inhabits the Cascade and Coast mountain ranges of North America, as well as the Rocky Mountain chain.

Now extinct but known from fossils found in caves of the American Southwest, the smaller *Oreamnos harringtoni* is the only other recognized past or present member of the mountain goat's genus. Fossil evidence suggests that during the massive Wisconsin Glaciation, both species of mountain goats survived only south of the continental ice sheet, even as far south as California and northern Mexico. Yet recent DNA analyses indicate that the coasts of northern British Columbia and southern Alaska provided additional refugia in which goats persisted until the Pleistocene ice melted away.

Is there a more elegant
beast? (Photo by author)

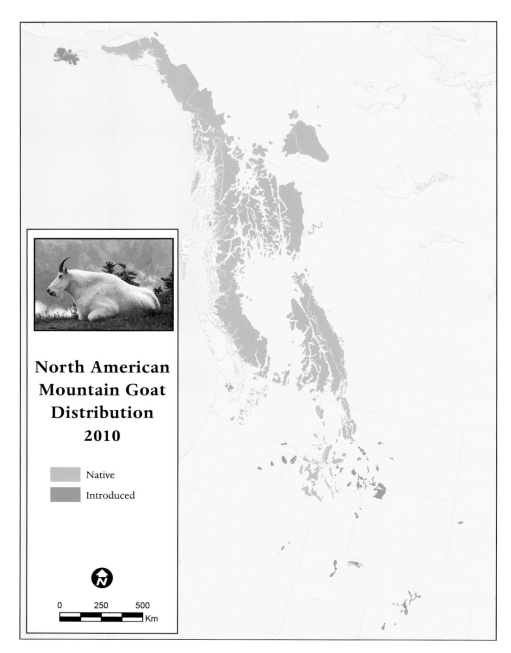

North American Mountain Goat Distribution 2010

Native

Introduced

0   250   500
Km

The continental distribution in 2010 of native and introduced populations of mountain goats (map and photo from the British Columbia Mountain Goat Management Plan, 2010).

The periglacial conditions that shaped *Oreamnos americanus* are what the species remains best adapted to today. It's found from southern Alaska to the western Northwest Territories and southward through Canada to Washington, Idaho, and Montana. Beyond this distribution of native populations, new herds have been established by transplanting animals to Colorado, Nevada, Oregon, Utah, eastern Idaho, central Montana, the Olympic Peninsula of Washington, several Alaskan islands, and even beneath the granite gaze of four presidents in the Black Hills of South Dakota.

CHAPTER TWO

How to Build a Goat

DOI: 10.5876_9781607322924.c002

The mountain goat is defined by the suite of traits that permit it to defy gravity twelve months a year. Specialization starts with the feet. The hard outer walls of the hooves surround a rough yet pliable, convex pad. The animal world's equivalent of studded tires, the hoof pads conform to rock surfaces providing positraction. The four "toes" (digits two and three comprising the cloven hoof, and digits one and four being the elevated "dew claws" on the rear of the foot) are oversized—a feature that affords a larger gripping surface and distributes the foot load for increased support on snow. The cloven hoof is more flexible than in other ungulates. As the goat descends a rocky face or steep snowfield, the toes spread apart improving balance and providing friction in an outward as well as downward direction. During descents, the goat lowers his hind quarters to bring the large dew claws into contact with rock and snow, increasing traction and control.

His overall build includes short, stocky legs set relatively close together, and a compact torso with the forequarters decidedly larger than the rear (*a la* McKenzie and Guthrie's "white buffler"). The heavily muscled shoulders and forelegs help him trudge through deep snow. A compact body provides a low center of gravity, balance, and uncanny agility on narrow ledges that vanish into thin air. When startled he may trot or lope, but this is not an animal built for speed.

Mountain goats are the smallest of all North American ungulate offspring, weighing only thirty-five to fifty pounds during their first winter. The beard and flowing pantaloons of its mother are already evident on this ten-month-old kid. (Photo by author)

Like a Spiderman of the cliffs, the mountain goat's feats are breathtaking, and in this case for just a lick of salt. (G. Dan Hutcheson, WildPhotons)

Two male bighorn sheep (*Ovis canadensis*), a distant relative of the mountain goat, share parts of the white climber's North American geographic range. (Photo by author)

Although nimble in the mountains by hoofed animal standards, North America's Dall, Stone, and bighorn sheep (collectively called mountain sheep) possess neither the physical adaptations nor the raw ability of the mountain goat on cliffs and crags. While sheep bound crisply across outcrops and slopes, the goat is a plodder and inclined to stick to steeper terrain. Leverage, friction, and balance are the tools of his trade. The sheep are free-climbing scramblers; the goat is a technician.

I've watched a goat climb to the top of a dizzying pinnacle and stand with all four feet together on a summit measuring only eight inches square. Then he raised a hind foot, scratched behind an ear, and shook the dust from his coat, unimpressed with the feat as I looked on in wonder.

The goat's outward appearance is marked by an extravagant robe of white. It's from late fall into spring that he looks his most elegant, highlighted by a full beard, pantaloons that resemble baggy basketball shorts, and a dorsal ridge of hair that when backlit casts a radiant halo befitting a beast living so close to the heavens. This outer pelage of five- to seven-inch-long guard hair sheds wind and snow and protects a dense insulating mantle of underfur (goats patented the concept of layering for warmth!) as luxurious as the finest cashmere. To my eye, they are among the most photogenic of subjects.

From May into August, goats metamorphose from this shaggy beast of winter into trimmer summer attire. Often last to shed is the guard hair of the pantaloons, scraggly remnants under the belly, and a goatee wisp of beard. With a fresh half-inch of wool adorning the rest of the body, the American mountain goat looks far from chic, if not comical, as the molt progresses. Only the Dall sheep of the far north shares an all white coat among ungulates. But unlike the goat, the sheep's closely cropped summer appearance changes little during winter.

When the goats began to shed their too-warm-for-summer dress in spring, indigenous peoples from Alaska to Washington plucked tufts of this fur found snagged on bushes. After twisting the wool into yarn, they wove blankets and garments prized for their beauty, comfort, and warmth.

The white coat reflects solar radiation, enabling goats to feed on exposed terrain, rather than seeking the coolness of forests in summer. Still, on August afternoons, they may retreat to the shade of cliffs or lounge on remnant snowfields to better thermoregulate and ease the aggravation of insect pests.

The color of the coat is not truly white, but a buttery ivory that contrasts with the snow, particularly when glistening in sunlight. Still, spotting these cliff-dwellers is challenging on a mountainside smothered or patchily covered in snow. Amid driving rain, snow squalls, and wind-driven graupel (all too common conditions on goat ranges), goats can vanish like ghosts in a fog.

Because his coat is not waterproof, the lee side of outcrops, overhangs, and caves offer refuge during particularly wet weather. Goat caves I've found in Montana's

From the moment they are born, kids
are imprinted on a vertical world and
take to it instinctively. (Photo by author)

Members of some First Nation tribes still collect shed mountain goat fur for weaving of luxurious garments and blankets. (Photo by author)

Goats do not shed their warm winter
coats until mid-summer. So like this
one, by May they seek the cool comfort
of snow and shade. (Photo by author)

This cave in Montana's Bitterroot Mountains offered a sanctuary for goats on particularly brutal winter days or to shelter them from rain. (Photo by author)

Bitterroot Range and in Glacier National Park were carpeted with a layer of decomposing dung.

Finally, this creamy attire is highlighted by a coal black nose, eyes, and dagger-like horns measuring eight to eleven inches long in adults. The horns are neither the spiraled variety of true goats, nor the dramatically curled and flared horns of mountain sheep. Still they serve as formidable weapons when the head is lowered to face any would-be attacker. They also constitute a prodigious reinforcement of an animal's rank in the mountain goat's social hierarchy. I'll return to this subject in the next chapter.

A finely tuned specialist, America's goat-antelope inhabits a realm where the vertical dimension supersedes all others. My persistently cocked head and uplifted binoculars attested to that. Although equipped with magnificent physical adaptations, the mental game is where goats may best excel. That became what I most admired during countless days watching these cliff walkers negotiate their vertical world.

Rock climbing requires a combination of strength, skill, and confidence (can-do attitude). To successfully spend a ten- to twelve-year life span on cliffs requires one other ingredient: patience. Natural selection and diligent parental training have given the mountain goat remarkable patience. Goats choose their routes. Their climbing is methodical, even painstaking. They are not averse to abandoning a route and seeking an alternative should the footing turn treacherous. Goats can perform "walk-overs" when a cliff ledge narrows to nothingness. A quick lurch to position his forefeet against the cliff face, followed by walking the feet above the head across the rock, and he's ambling back along the ledge nibbling sedges and groundsels.

While studying mountain goats in Montana's Bitterroot Mountains, again and again I was amazed by their patience. High on the cliffs one winter day, I stalked a nanny I wanted to immobilize with my dart gun and then radio-collar. I planned my stalk from the canyon bottom to the ledge where she was feeding, some 1,000 feet of elevation above me. An hour later, she and I met on the ledge. Startled, she bounded out of sight before I could get off a shot. I waited several minutes and then followed. Just beyond an angle in the cliff where the ledge ended in a seventy-five-foot vertical drop, she stood facing me. I couldn't immobilize her there for fear she would plummet from the ledge when she lost control of her limbs. So I retreated some fifty yards and sat, dart gun ready, behind a boulder. Surely she would retrace her steps and I'd dart her as she passed by. Three hours later, with the sun sinking into Idaho, my hands and feet numb, and *my* patience played out, she remained at the same location. I bid her good night before descending in the twilight. The next morning I spotted her grazing near the boulder where I had waited.

Seldom in a hurry, the mountain goat's climbing is calculated, even painstaking, a trait that serves it well on the cliffs. (Photo by author)

Again and again as I watched them, feats unthinkable to other large mammals proved routine for these alpine athletes. (Photo by author)

A lone goat on a wall of rock in Glacier National Park, Montana. How did he get there, and why? (Photo by author)

A nanny and her ten-month-old kid, where they're
typically seen—somewhere above. (Photo by author)

I was once asked: if I could come back to this world as an animal, what kind would
I choose? "If you mean a mammal," I replied, "I'd be a mountain goat." Besides being
able to survive in those spectacular surroundings, I'd prize being granted that kind of
patience.

Even on wet surfaces, the white climber's hooves provide extraordinary traction. (Photo by author)

When summer comes to the alpine zone, goats dine on a smorgasbord of plant life. (Photo by author)

CHAPTER THREE

Behaving Appropriately

DOI: 10.5876/9781607322924.c003

The mountain goat is one of the ruminants—the even-toed, hoofed mammals with complex stomachs where food is fermented by bacteria and protozoans to wring sparse nutrients from plants. Their digestive efficiency permits mountain goats to eat a variety of fibrous plants in winter when the availability of nutritious green forage is limited in temperate and subarctic regions. Although a specialist in many ways, the goat is a generalist in diet. Like most adaptations, this is a behavioral trait borne of necessity.

During much of the year—November into May—snow suffocates their world. On canyon walls, where cliffs and crags face a southerly slanting sun, goats search the ledges and slopes for sparse patches of food. Winter after winter they repeatedly graze and browse plants at the windward edges of ledges, where snow depths are shallower.

The specific composition of their catholic diet varies with snow depth, with stage of growth or curing of each plant, and with plant composition across the mountain goat's continental range. Like wooly veg-o-matics, they paw through snow for grasses and sedges, nibble mosses and lichens from rocks, strip twigs from shrubs and trees, and sometimes dig the rhizomes of ground-hugging plants. On some Rocky Mountain ranges of

Kids remain with their mothers for a year, and sometimes longer. The strong bond between a nanny and her offspring ensures that during their first year of life, kids learn what plants to eat and where to find them, migratory routes to seasonal ranges, and other necessities of a life on the rocks. (Photo by author)

Colorado and elsewhere, wind sweeps the snow from shreds of tall ridges, and goats may outlast winter nibbling on dwarfed alpine plants at sky-scraping elevations. In Alaska and British Columbia's coastal ranges—where snow piles higher than a house—goats descend far down the mountains (even to the seashore) and strip lichens from ancient trees in the dark depths of winter. Wherever they roam, mountain goats make do with what they can find. Winter is a period of energy conservation and waiting—waiting for the season of renewal, waiting for spring.

Although finding tasty plants likely enhances a mountain goat's energy balance and survival, filling one's stomach is the first order of business when snow buries the land. I once watched a nanny goat in a Bitterroot canyon mangle a seven-foot-tall serviceberry bush—a preferred dietary shrub. All the lower branches, which would have been more tender and nutritious than the thumb-thick main stem, had been stripped by past browsing. She mouthed the main stem, twisted and tugged until finally she snapped it three feet above the ground. Then she munched each of the lateral twigs and finally ate part of the coarse main stem. Consuming small branches that have blown to the ground from ponderosa pine and Douglas fir trees are other instances where feeding efficiency wins out over searching and snow-plowing for more digestible morsels. Such behavior promotes energy conservation by reducing time spent foraging that burns the body's precious fat stores.

Goats live in a matriarchal society—a pecking order dominated by females that is common to species as diverse as bees, bonobo chimps, and elephants. Adult females (called nannies) command the highest social rank followed by subadults (two-year-olds and yearlings) and kids (those less than a year old). Among nannies, social rank increases with age. This dominance hierarchy is persistently reinforced with a complex repertoire of stares, postures, and threats—escalating degrees of aggression—that are well understood by all (see *A Beast the Color of Winter* for behavioral details). And this aggression is not spread evenly among all individuals. Adult nannies are by far the bossiest goats, as much as ten times more than adult males, who are called billies.

Kids weigh just thirty-five to fifty pounds in winter (smaller than any other North American ungulate during its first winter) which renders them lowest on the pecking order and challenged to travel and forage effectively in deep snow. A kid remains with its mother until its first birthday (and sometimes until its second), nibbling food from the craters the nanny paws in the snow, gaining a measure of warmth bedded beside her, and enjoying her steadfast protection against carnivores seeking a meal of goat veal. Although the oldest and largest goats win most social conflict encounters, kids

A semi-stable social group that includes two yearlings with an adult nanny and her kid. (Photo by author)

Always seeking a room with a view, goats use traditional bedsites from which they can watch for dangers and maybe just admire their surroundings. (Photo by author)

fortuitously enjoy a measure of security from bullying by others when tucked beside their domineering mothers.

This quite stable, age-linear, dominance hierarchy among bands of adult females, their offspring, and subadults—commonly called nursery groups—is less predictable among males. As juvenile males mature, they grow more aggressive and challenge even adult nannies on occasion. As they reach about three years of age, males leave nursery groups and spend the remainder of their lives wandering singly or in small bachelor groups. Among themselves, billies too establish and maintain a linear hierarchy based on social rank, largely related to their age and increasing body size.

Except during the fall rut, billies interact little with nannies and nursery groups. When they do, adult males—which easily outweigh all other members of the herd—appear conflicted and often behave submissively. This response may be a product of their ritualized courtship behavior in which males passively tend females and approach prospective mates with utmost caution until females enter estrous and no longer rebuke their suitors' advances.

On canyon cliffs in the depths of winter (December to April), I've watched females and even subadults rebuff adult billies with a horn threat or even a charge when the males encounter nursery groups. More often, mutual avoidance maintains personal space and order. Across many goat ranges adult males occupy peripheral areas of the winter habitat. They more often use forested areas than others, whereas nannies seek out the more snow-free and secure feeding and bedding crags.

In truth, the larger and more powerful billies (150–200 pounds compared to about 125–140 pounds for adult females in the lower forty-eight states, though as much as 50 percent larger to the north) can handle deeper snow and don't share the burden of nurturing offspring or nourishing a growing fetus. What may appear as less optimal habitat may actually afford adult males more or higher quality food. Males continue to gain structural size and body mass until seven or eight years of age. Good nutrition can help a billy survive to old age, which boosts his social rank and increases opportunities to breed and pass on his genes—the paramount pay-off of male dominance. Whereas males may select habitat that enhances nutrition, even at higher risk of predation, females seek the security of steeper, more predator-free terrain, which presumably enhances survival of their offspring.

As products of their local environment, as well as their genes, their sociability and use of habitat are not immutably set in stone across their North American distribution. Where populations occur at higher densities, and especially where goats congregate during summer at natural salt licks (a relished, limited, and defensible resource) adult billies may be winners more often than other goats during aggressive interactions. On goat ranges where densities are high, or food occurs in larger patches (because terrain is less broken and steep), and again when goats gather at mineral licks, group sizes of ten

An adult nanny, kid, and two-year-old female. (Photo by author)

During the November mating season, an adult billy patiently tends a nanny with her kid of last spring. (Photo by author)

or more animals are not uncommon. This is the case on many goat ranges of interior northern British Columbia and parts of Alberta. Yet coastal goat populations of British Columbia and Alaska live a lifestyle in winter that's more reminiscent of their Asian relatives, the gorals and serows. Bound to pockets of steep country on densely timbered slopes, they endure soggy snows of maritime winters in low density populations, socializing in groups that average less than three animals.

Turning to native goat ranges south of Canada—which are broadly rugged, steep, and lightly forested—group sizes tend to be small, averaging only two to three animals. In this vertical world where soil's a scarce commodity, food is spotty, and where life embraces cracks and ledges, survival is tenuous. Competition for space is intense and personal space is well defended.

Whereas goats stick to rugged terrain for security, more social ungulates use open habitats with more continuous food patches, relying on foot speed and herding of animals as protection from predators. Even in the loose associations of nanny and subadult groups—whose members may be closely related—tolerance has its limits. Invading an adult nanny's personal space of six to ten feet often results in a threatening response, if only a ritualized posture that translates as "back off." The rich body language of goat society promotes avoidance of physical contact and especially stabs from those potentially lethal horns. In over 95 percent of all contests observed in both Canadian and American behavioral studies, goats were able to decide whose rank and personal space was preeminent without resorting to physical contact.

Beyond the danger of puncture wounds, aggressive interactions may cause other injury to the white climbers. In 4,400 hours of observing goats in northwest Montana, Douglas Chadwick recorded almost 300 agonistic encounters between goats on steep terrain. Of thirty-nine encounters in which goats fell or lost their footing, eighteen goats were "directly pushed, prodded or knocked over the edge; eighteen others were forced to make a frantic leap to escape and lacked adequate footing to land on; and the remainder were either innocent bystanders bumped off a ledge by battling goats, or a case of the aggressor slipping in haste."

My observations in the Bitterroots showed that goats' intolerance for sharing their personal space escalated with the steepness of terrain. I gasped as goats sometimes forced others off narrow ledges in falls up to twenty vertical feet, with no apparent harm. But even goats can sometimes make unforced errors, as in the deaths of five animals that naturalist Ernest Thompson Seton observed fall to their deaths from a dead-end ledge.

Compared with other North American hoofed mammals, mountain goat society appears unruly. In Alberta, biologists Francois Fournier and Marco Festa-Bianchet learned that adult nannies typically take part in three to four conflicts with other goats per hour. By comparison, the more socially well-adjusted bighorn sheep—which live

On a sunny day an adult billy snoozes in a bed of snow. (Photo by author)

Goats prefer secure bedsites, even if that means having to brace oneself to keep from sliding into oblivion. (Photo by author)

on nearby mountains—will clash just once every two to three hours during the rutting season when aggression is highest.

Despite appearances, I believe this system of well-ordered and measured belligerence has evolved over the millennia to serve mountain goats well. A social structure typified by constant threats, bluff charges, and sporadic clashes limits group sizes and competition for prime feeding sites in a vertical world where food is spotty—mere snacks on precarious shelves. This spacing of animals across rugged real estate prevents a population from over-using its food supply and forestalls stress and disease that can accompany over-crowding.

During summer and fall, aggression relaxes—the consequence of abundant food, less environmental stress, and goats using less precipitous terrain. Where topography permits, Canadian scientists Steeve Côté and Marco Festa-Bianchet suggest that larger groupings of goats may serve as an anti-predator strategy. More eyes and ears guard against a sneak attack by a lion or wolf; and the intimidation effect of a crowd dissuades all but the most resolute carnivore. Regardless of the relative abundance of predators or risk of predation on mountain goat ranges, greater social tolerance facilitates more animals foraging on prime feeding sites to nourish their young and recover body condition for the upcoming winter.

At its core, the goat is both product and captive of its evolutionary history and specialization as a mountain climber. But the specifics of these cliff-dwellers' habitat use and social behavior are attuned to the vicissitudes of the seasons and which rocks they roam.

Mountain goats are polygamous, meaning males may breed several mates; but they do not gather harems like elk do, for example. Individuals first become sexually active when they reach two-and-a-half years of age—but may not breed until a year or two older—whereas many other North American ungulates first mate as yearlings or two-year-olds. Beginning in November and through early December, billies search for females. Older males court females by forming consort pairs. Each may "tend" one or more nannies one at a time, defending each from other males until she becomes receptive to his advances. While tending a female not yet in estrus, a billy spends much time simply watching over her and feeding very little. Younger males may seek breeding opportunities by chasing, or "coursing," females. But this is rarely successful behavior as dominant males drive off the upstarts, and females may not accept them.

In romance too, patience is virtuous. Submissive posturing is proper etiquette as billies cautiously approach and sniff females to determine their reproductive status. Females not in estrus will threaten or charge their suitors once their personal space is

Goats on parade! (Photo by author)

Bighorn sheep prefer less rugged habitat than the mountain goat, though they are sympatric in parts of the Rocky Mountain chain. (Photo by author)

Among ungulates, mountain goats are not known for their vocalizations. This billy uttered a soft bleat as I approached. (Photo by author)

An adult nanny being courted by a billy in December. (Photo by author)

Mountain goats are fond of dust bathing to provide relief from biting insects, although the coolness of moist soil is often favored in summer. These comfort activities are different from the ritualized behavior in which males dig shallow rutting pits in late fall. (Photo by author)

violated. Patience not only is chivalrous but also may avert a painful poke from a nanny's rapier headgear.

Rutting pits dug by males are a ritualized aspect of courtship behavior. After pawing the ground, a billy will sit like a dog in the shallow depression and paw soil onto his hind quarters and belly. Accordingly, breeding-age males are distinguishable by their dirty coats. Males also rub their horns against vegetation where sticky secretions from the crescent-shaped horn glands advertise a billy's presence.

Like so much of the mountain goat's hard-wired behavior, displays of size and social status—rather than outright conflict involving contact—are customary between competing billies. Contrary to mountain sheep and most species of true goats that battle head to head, mountain goats circle antiparallel so that horn strikes are most often landed in the hind quarters or flanks. Natural selection has countered this hazardous behavior by growing a dermal shield over the goat's hind quarters. This tough area of skin may reach an inch in thickness.

Despite these behavioral and physical constraints, their horns can be lethal weapons with instances recorded of dead goats bearing a dozen or more puncture wounds. These could result from male combat or from a nanny's retaliation of an unwelcome suitor's inappropriate advances. In a mating system in which males submissively court and dutifully tend females, experience favors those who have learned proper protocol. In one study researchers found that 91 percent of females were bred by high ranking, older males.

With mating accomplished, females, their kids, and subadults travel to favored areas of winter range. Males wander off to spend much of winter solitarily or in small bachelor groups.

DOI: 10.5876_9781607732924.c004

CHAPTER FOUR

Rewards and Risks

A life spent living on ledges and peaks comes with both rewards and risks. Few other hoofed mammals spend significant time where the mountain goat roams, finding life easier on more forgiving terrain. During my observations I found that only mule deer and more rarely elk shared the Bitterroot haunts of mountain goats. In other goat ranges, mountain sheep also overlap their distribution and may vie for forage. But of all North America's large herbivores, the mountain goat and musk ox exist most freely from interspecific competition for food and space—a reward of sorts of their desolate domains.

Likewise, most predators lack the tenacity or mountaineering skills to hunt this sure-footed climber. Those that occasionally kill goats are bears, wolves, mountain lions, and even wolverines and eagles. Where predation has been quantified, grizzlies and wolves are the most significant predators of goats. In an Alberta study, kids and yearlings were most vulnerable.

On thin ledges, bears and wolves are not much of a threat. But where goats stray from steep terrain, and especially where heaps of wet snow force them to descend to coastal Alaska and British Columbia's old growth forests, bears and wolves more readily dine on mountain goat fare.

Elk typically prefer forests and meadows, like the group of cows and calves here, rather than the rugged country used by mountain goats. (Photo by Diana Stratton)

Every spring hundreds of thousands of elk (Cervus elaphus) migrate to summer ranges in the mountains of the West. (Photo by the author)

Black bears (*Ursus americanus*) cruise the more gentle terrain on goat ranges and scavenge on winter-killed animals, often where carcasses have been deposited by avalanches. (Photo by author)

A common carnivore in rugged terrain, and the predator probably best adapted for preying on the mountain goat, is the mountain lion or cougar (*Puma concolor*). It can reach 200 pounds in weight. (Glacier National Park archives)

The golden eagle (*Aquila chrysaetos*) is a powerfully built bird of prey capable of batting a young goat from a cliff. (© Ganesh K. Jayaraman)

Coyotes (*Canis latrans*) are both predators and scavengers. Their prey largely consists of much smaller species than the winter-killed elk that this one is scavenging. (Photo by author)

The mountain lion is large and powerful enough to bring down the white mountaineer. And it's the predator most often found prowling goat-rugged terrain. As lion numbers have increased in recent decades, predation on goats may also have risen.

The fifteen-pound golden eagle, on the other hand—though a fierce hunter of smaller mammals and birds—seems unsuited for killing prey the size of goats. Indeed, it picks its targets carefully, seeking young kids to carry away or to strike and knock from cliff ledges. After gravity has done its work, the eagle feeds on its fallen victims below the cliffs. Bald eagles have also attacked young goats.

To counter the eagle, nannies tuck their young beneath them when the large bird soars overhead. Even the shadow of a raven or red-tailed hawk may cause a mother to shield a newborn with those stiletto horns held at the ready. This protective behavior of nannies probably limits the vulnerability of kids, unless they are left unguarded. The consensus from ecological studies suggests that eagle predation is of limited consequence to the wellbeing of goat herds.

The most common predator on many goat ranges south of Canada is the coyote, and this was true of the Bitterroots as well. Most often I spotted them coursing terrain below the cliffs, mousing or seeking the remains of winter-killed goats to scavenge. During February 1974, I peered anxiously through my spotting scope as one harassed a nanny and kid. The coyote repeatedly attempted to dissociate the pair by seemingly daring the nanny to charge. When the nanny dropped her headgear into assault position and obliged, the coyote dashed aside and cut behind her. Nevertheless, she recovered each time to chase the coyote from her kid and eventually routed him. In another instance, a pair of coyotes confronted a nanny and kid on the narrowest stretch of ledge. The nanny stood over her youngster and simply waited the coyotes out. Patience and perseverance again proved defining traits of the mountain goat.

When it comes to self-defense, the mountain goat is clearly no pushover against even larger adversaries than the coyote. Observations by Steeve Côté and colleagues at Caw Ridge, Alberta, evidenced goats escaping attacks by grizzly bears, wolves, and a wolverine. In one misfire, an adult wolf successfully grabbed a three-month-old kid from a group of fifty-two goats that were feeding on gentle terrain. The kid's mother immediately charged the wolf. After she struck him in the hindquarters twice, the wolf apparently reassessed the situation and released the kid unharmed.

As limited as the threat of predation in their vertical world may be, this has not dulled the white climber's attentiveness to danger. Mountain goats have evolved patterned behaviors that enhance security on the cliffs, as Montana goat researcher Douglas Chadwick explained:

A nanny shelters her week-
old offspring while keeping
a wary eye on another adult
goat below. (Photo by author)

The normal activities of mountain goats are interspersed with behavior patterns that
have developed as anti-predator adaptations. These include: the habit of raising the
head to look around at intervals while feeding, a proclivity for walking on the outside

A typically secure bedsite chosen by
a mountain goat, this one in Idaho's
Palisades Wilderness Area. (Photo by author)

More often than not, a mountain goat will enjoy a deep yawn after settling onto a bed site. Stretching, scratching, and licking one's coat are other comfort activities intermixed with ruminating and dozing while bedded. (Photo by author)

Besides peering over precipices to inspect their surroundings, goats venture to the brink of snow cornices to peruse what may lurk below. (Photo by author)

edges of ledges and overhanging snow cornices to gain a better view of the situation below, pausing on high vantage points during feeding and travelling to gaze for long periods of time and test the wind before going on, the selection of bedsites that over-look the landscape and have a high wall behind them, a routine of carefully surveying their surroundings for several minutes before bedding down, and rising and turning every half hour or so to scan the terrain anew and then re-bedding to face a different direction than before (though this is probably for the sake of relieving stiffness too).

But starvation in winter and the mountains themselves may claim more goats than do predators. The drain of deep snow on foraging success, severe weather's effects on newborn survival, and inevitable accidents that accompany a life defying gravity take a cumulative toll on these cliff-dwellers.

During my three years in the Bitterroots I found the remains of twelve goats that had died. Three I found at the base of cliffs where falls or snowslides may have deposited them. But due to scavenging or advanced decomposition, I couldn't be sure of the reason that any had met their end. They averaged 10.8 years of age at death, with females rang-ing from 8.5 to 13.5 and males from 6.5 to 15.5. The smaller and more fragile bodies and bones of young animals make it less likely that their remains would persist long enough to be discovered. Yet my population surveys showed that kids (31 percent) and yearlings (23 percent) suffered the highest annual losses from natural causes—a pattern also noted by every other biologist who has studied the animal. Protracted winters can take a much higher toll when more than half of all kids may not reach their first birthday.

Although an eighteen-year-old female and a fourteen-year-old male were reported from a collection of 165 skulls in a Canadian museum, most field studies concur that goats rarely surpass twelve or thirteen years of age in the wild. A two-decade study of an unhunted goat herd at Alberta's Caw Ridge found that annual survival (the probability of animals surviving for one year) was 94 percent for females aged two through nine but just 76 percent after age nine. Throughout their lives, nannies had a better chance than billies of surviving each year once they had reached one year of age. This tendency for females to outlive males is a life history characteristic of most large mammals.

Many of the skulls I examined at taxidermy shops of goats ten and older had severely worn, loose, or missing incisiform teeth (the six incisors and two incisor-shaped canines at the front of the lower jaw used for clipping vegetation). Others had chipped incisors, possibly products of climbing accidents. Bad teeth compromise foraging efficiency—a goat's ability to crop grasses, clip twigs, and peel plant morsels from rocks and crevices. Along with debilitating injuries, failing teeth limit the maximum lifespan of most large mammals. Thus, mortality of goats from natural causes follows the general mammalian pattern of higher mortality for both juvenile and very old individuals with relatively low death rates for prime breeding-aged adults.

A nanny in her element of snow. This one's right eye appeared white and opaque. She walked with her head cocked as if to better watch where she was going, suggesting she was blind in that eye. (Photo by author)

The unforgiving conditions of their mountain retreat shielded mountain goats from the nineteenth-century Euro-American decimation of much western wildlife. But for that reprieve, there is a price to pay. Throughout its western range observers recount that even this ace of alpinists is subject to missteps and tumbles. I once watched in horror as a nanny and kid, while attempting to turn around, both fell fifteen feet from a dead-end sliver of ledge. The kid landed upright, unharmed. The nanny was not so fortunate. She crashed back-first onto a juniper bush, inflicting a nasty wound on her foreleg. This is a cost of a life on steep rocks, where security and danger are oddly intertwined.

As a measure of injury suffered from social aggression and climbing accidents, I measured horn breakage in a sample of 123 Bitterroot goats harvested by hunters from 1973 to 1978. On 30 percent, one or both horns were broken. However, 70 percent of all horn breakage had occurred by the time goats had reached three-and-a-half years old. Douglas Chadwick's meticulous observations of mountain goats in northwestern Montana confirmed that younger goats are more vulnerable to falls. Eighty percent of all climbing accidents brought on by social aggression were suffered by kids and yearlings. Experience, strength, and senior position in the social hierarchy may all buffer older animals from becoming casualties of the mountain itself—but only if they survive long enough.

Life at altitude exposes goats to the howling, skull-numbing gales of winter. But as we've seen, these Ice Age survivors possess the physical adaptations, and the attitude, to weather such conditions. Yet when snow buries the mountain, the search for sparse food tests and weakens even the toughest, particularly in years when winter drags far into spring. Failing nutrition of half-the-year winters is among the risks of living yearlong in their kingdom of white.

In April I found goats probing the lowest elevations of the Bitterroot canyons. That's when the first sprigs of bluegrass and buttercups greened the south-facing slopes where winter-weary goats had spent the past six months. This was the good news that marked their release from a nutritionally deficient subsistence. Highly digestible, protein-rich new growth halted the decline of body condition and was essential for pregnant nannies to bear a new generation in need of rich milk. Yet early spring was a time marked by the bad and the ugly, as well as the good.

Late snow storms cheat spring by burying any flush of new growth, a circumstance that can push some malnourished animals over the edge. More dramatically, spring can be the most treacherous time of year for young and old, male and female alike. This is the season of the ugly, of thundering avalanches. When conditions are right, the sliding of snow is an awesome spectacle on goat winter ranges. During the day, exposed rock

(*Facing page*) It can sometimes be easier to spot their tracks in winter than the mountain goats that made them. How many animals do you see here?
(Photo by author)

(*There are six.*)

Goats often hazard peering over the edge of snow cornices, or in this case the randkluft where a chasm gapes between the adjoining rock headwall at a glacier's upper margin. (Photo by author)

absorbs solar energy and melts adjacent snow, which flows and freezes under large snow-fields. Fluctuation of temperatures around the freezing point causes slabs of snow, both small and immense, to slide off ledges, crash over cliffs, and plunge down debris chutes, carrying ice, rock, and trees along for the ride. This would seem a bad time to live on a cliff.

In fact, the shedding of snow by the mountains is both a blessing and a curse. Avalanches expose new patches of food to hungry goats; but they may also claim their lives. Many researchers have found the battered remains of goats in avalanche debris. The carcasses serve as carrion for bears, coyotes, ravens, eagles, and other scavengers.

Goats live in a noisy environment: wind, running water, and persistent rockfall are the white noise of the cliffs. Goats often pay little attention to such sounds, as they are as normal as ocean breakers on a beach. But when an avalanche rumbles down the mountain, goats scramble against rock walls or duck under cliff overhangs. Their panic is palpable.

Thus, the Old Man of the Mountains pays a price for his precarious security. This paradox of his niche reminds me of a description in *Wild Delicate Seconds* of seventeen snowy owls that Charles Finn watched serenely perched on fence posts one wintry day: "Resigned to the vagaries of fate and hopeful about the carelessness of mice, they were waiting out their portion of eternity with exceptional calm." Substituting the words "carelessness of winter" for "carelessness of mice," renders an apt description of the mountain goat's life.

The hoary marmot, a twelve-pound rodent with which the mountain goat's distribution most closely coincides, avoids the perils of winter by hibernating from October to June. Far beneath winter's white blanket he burns stored fat manufactured from last summer's crop of glacier lilies and sheep fescue. He never hears the avalanches that thunder down the mountains as the goats hunker against the cliffs.

After marmots emerge from eight months of slumber and goats roam to the high cirques and ridges of their range, both feast upon giant salad bowls of nutrient-rich grasses, sedges, groundsels, and other alpine delicacies. These two species have prospered on the summits with differing lifestyles, yet both are distinctively harmonized with the mountains' vicissitudes.

Avalanches are a powerful force that sweeps rock and trees and occasionally goats down the mountainsides. (Photo by author)

The remains of an unfortunate billy goat I found
in an avalanche run-out. It had already been
scavenged by coyotes and a black bear when I
discovered it in May. (Photo by author)

Following eight months of hibernation, a hoary marmot (*Marmota caligata*) peeks from her underground burrow. (Photo by author)

Among the earliest blooming plants, phlox (*Phlox diffusa*) is a harbinger of spring on goat winter ranges in the Rockies. (Photo by author)

One of the loveliest spring blooms
on mountain goat ranges is the
delicate pasqueflower (*Anemone
patens*). (Photo by author)

DOI: 10.5876_9781607322924.c005

CHAPTER FIVE

Among the Goats

During three decades of field studies of North America's large mammals, the environmental and logistical challenges of none—not deer, elk, moose, pronghorn, bighorn sheep, or bears—compared with those I encountered learning about the mountain goat. The chasms and ramparts, the remoteness and weather are both physically and mentally taxing. Other field biologists have discovered the same, some under the harshest of conditions or across expanses of time.

Stewart Brandborg was among the first to observe and record details of the mountain goat's life. From 1947 through 1952, he surveyed the animal across a swath of its Montana and Idaho distribution, then he composed a classic monograph on the animal's natural history. Douglas and Beth Chadwick spent three winters (1972 to 1974) encamped on a bleak goat range near Montana's Bob Marshall Wilderness. With remarkable diligence, they recorded the behavior and fortunes of several bands of white climbers during the yearly ice age. For a dozen years, Douglas Houston, Bruce Morehead, and a cadre of colleagues studied the introduced goats of Olympic National Park, where controversy swirled around their exotic but charismatic status. And beginning in 1989, Marco Festa-Bianchet, Steeve Côté, and associates initiated the longest-running study of the animal's ecology and behavior at Alberta's Caw Ridge. Others too, from Alaska to Colorado, have toiled and delighted to better understand the goat's unique existence so that it might remain an enduring wilderness icon.

My own efforts began with forays into Bitterroot canyons out of curiosity about the animal. During that first winter of 1972–73, I often pitched my pup tent miles up some desolate gash in their granite stronghold. Single-digit temperatures and snow-bound landscapes are incomparable instructors. Stuffing my compact gas stove in the sleeping bag along with my boots—so that the former cold-hearted gadget might be persuaded to heat water for a breakfast of tea and instant oatmeal, and the latter might forestall frostbitten toes—were lessons quickly learned in wilderness bushcraft.

But backpacking winter camps gobbled time that detracted from finding the subjects I sought to study. So in fall 1973, my graduate program advisor Dr. Bart O'Gara and I hauled a slide-in camper into Fred Burr Canyon. We off-loaded it near the end of a crude track that had been excluded from inclusion when the Selway-Bitterroot Wilderness Area was demarcated in 1964. Though a mere seven feet long and just four feet high, the camper provided a solid roof over my head, a cot, propane space heater, and two-burner stove. It served as operational center and refuge for me, and for the shrews that relentlessly infested the place. From this base camp, I conducted my research in Fred Burr and adjacent canyons, each of which supported herds of a handful to three dozen of the Bitterroots' native mountaineers. This was the backdrop for the final two years of my modest contribution to our understanding of this mystical beast's life on the rocks.

From repeated observations, I came to recognize certain goats in Fred Burr and other canyons. Unique horn characteristics identified some individuals. One I named Captain Hook for the sharply curved horns that graced the crown of this particularly robust billy. Another was Nubs, who I first observed in 1973 as a yearling. Both her horns were broken and round knobs had formed on the stubs. In my third year of observation, and her third year of life, she bore her first puffball kid.

In Fred Burr I supplemented my behavioral observations of Nubs, Captain Hook, and several distinctive others with three animals I radio-instrumented. Many researchers have captured and marked mountain goats, often with radio-collars, to monitor their movements to seasonal ranges and to determine if they return to ranges in successive years (behavior termed *range fidelity*). I was one of those biologists and tried two techniques to capture animals.

In November 1973, I constructed two Clover traps—a cage trap originally designed by wildlife biologist Melvin Clover in the 1950s to capture deer, one at a time. Each was

Goat cliffs above the author's winter camp in Fred Burr Canyon. (Photo by author)

Complete with picnic table and clothes line, the camper where the author spent two winters in the Bitterroot Mountains. (Photo by author)

I could identify a number of goats by their broken or unique horn characteristics. The yearling on the left I named Nubs for her stubby horns that she likely broke in a fall. (Photo by author)

a steel-framed enclosure draped in heavy jute netting that measured 7 feet by 3 feet by 4 feet high. At one end was a door that could be raised and connected to a trip line inside, which would trigger the door to drop behind it when a goat entered the trap. I somehow convinced college friends to help haul each of these—one completely constructed, the other in pieces (a much less grueling and dangerous choice, as it turned out)—1,000 vertical feet up the goat cliffs of Fred Burr Canyon. We placed fifty-pound salt blocks at favored bedding sites and after several weeks, I returned to place the Clover traps over the salt blocks, assuming this had given the goats enough time to become hooked on sodium chloride.

Across many goat ranges the animals are habituated to natural salt licks and seeps. Mineral licks in British Columbia draw animals as much as fifteen miles on traditional trails that traverse vast forested lands. The most famous may be the Walton Goat Lick on the southern border of Montana's Glacier National Park. There, dozens of the park's goats make daily pilgrimages in late spring and summer to slake their taste for naturally concentrated salt on a steep bank above the Flathead River. Formerly they made harrowing crossings of Montana's State Highway 2 to access the mineral lick, creating a hazard for motorists and to themselves. In 1981 reconstruction of the highway incorporated two underpasses, which Glacier's goats readily adopted as passageways to the Walton Goat Lick.

Unlike Glacier Park and some other goat ranges, the Bitterroots were not born of sedimentary rock containing carbonates and other salt concentrations, but rather granitic stone of igneous origin. No natural lick sites occurred. Although I sometimes saw goats licking the underside of ledges, they may have been doing so to sip water or scrape crustose lichens from the rock. Across the Bitterroot Valley in the Sapphire Mountains, another goat researcher trapped animals at a natural lick that he supplemented with hauled-in blocks of salt. He had considered a study area in the Bitterroots, but abandoned that choice due to the inhospitable terrain and lack of goat-attracting salt sites. As it turned out, the Bitterroot goats cared not enough about salt to enter my Clover traps.

My backup plan was to stalk goats in winter, sneaking close enough to inject them with a muscle immobilizing drug shot from a dart gun. Rather than capture them in summer, when the weather is more agreeable even at 8,000 to 10,000 feet elevation, I chose the depths of winter. Winter was when goats retreated to discreet ranges of the Bitterroots' many canyons.

My world was the canyon bottoms, each of which was followed by a rock-strewn Forest Service trail; their world loomed 600 to 1,500 feet above the streams grinding away the cliffs' foundations. It was a given that each attempt to capture animals would require mountaineering skills matching those of my quarry—an obvious conclusion from my first sighting of Bitterroot goats, three white specks clinging to a granite wall. The trick

In late June, mountain goats seeking natural salt deposits on the cliffs of the Walton Goat Lick above the turbulent waters of the Middle Fork Flathead River, Glacier National Park. (Photo by author)

Kamook, the wonder pup, on his first trip into the Bitterroot Mountains in March 1974. **(Photo by author)**

was to spot an animal in a place where I could approach it. The mountain goat's inborn allies of discretion and patience became mine as well.

In over two dozen attempts to dart Bitterroot goats, I succeeded in capturing but three. After several arduous, out-of-sight stalks, my quarry had sometimes vanished from lofty perches where I'd spotted them an hour or more earlier. More often, a roundabout approach across couloirs and thin ledges found my objective in a place where I dare not squeeze the trigger. Had I done so, a magnificent beast may have plunged to its death once the immobilizing drug took effect.

Sometimes accompanied by fellow graduate students or friends, but most often alone in the wilderness canyons, I chose a constant companion for my second winter in the wilderness. A mirror image of the cliff-dwellers I admired, I brought a Samoyed pup on his first trip to my winter camp when he was but fourteen weeks old. I named him Kamook, translated as dog from the language of the Chinook Tribe from whom Meriwether Lewis and William Clark had acquired their mountain goat hide. A breed bred for Arctic

The author radio-collaring an immobilized nanny
as his Samoyed pup looks on. (Courtesy, Jim Reichel)

conditions, the fifty-five degree temperature of my cramped camper proved too toasty for him. Kam preferred burrowing outside in the snow, and then pawed at the door for his breakfast when I stirred to brew coffee.

At the age of four and a half months he began trailing me up the goat cliffs. Not always fond of the places I scrambled to capture goats or to measure their feeding prefer-ences, I sometimes had to boost my timid companion up steep pitches.

I once descended an icy outcrop to a broad ledge thirty feet below and found myself alone. Kamook, the wonder pup, protested pitifully from a bleak slice of mountain above. No encouragement could convince him that his life was not in peril. So I rock-climbed back up to where he paced and whimpered. We were still 500 hundred feet up the mountain; night was closing in; and there was no better route down. With a length of parachute cord I kept stashed in my rucksack, I cinched a loop behind his front legs. His look told all: the end must be near. Despite his protestations, I lowered him down, loosed the cord and followed after. Wonder pup was never quite as trusting of me on the cliffs after that.

On the rare occasions he saw them, the goats were mysterious, even intimidating to Kam. During the one stalk with him that ended in success, he remained a safe distance and watched while I adorned the nanny with a radio collar.

From late December through April, the goats' lives settled into a fairly predictable routine of feeding, bedding, and scanning their domain. My life mimicked this simple pattern: feeding, bedding, and observing goats. The difference was that my surveillance required burning heaps of calories to hike or snowshoe (depending on conditions) to find them, making counts of animals in each canyon, and recording their distributions and behaviors. Kam would have been satisfied to stay closer to home—covering just the five-mile stretch of winter range in Fred Burr Canyon. But, oh no, his owner just had to venture elsewhere. So a day in Bear Canyon or Blodgett Canyon meant a trek out of Fred Burr, a drive to a trailhead, an eight-mile roundtrip trek into another canyon, then a return slog to our Fred Burr camp. An occasional night in the twelve-foot travel trailer of friends at the mouth of Fred Burr canyon saved us from trudging home in the dark.

Back at camp, a hearty meal of canned or dried goods was followed by reviewing and polishing the day's notes, a cup of cocoa, and sleep as profound as I've ever known. Occasionally the goats would visit me as I snuggled in my sleeping bag. They clattered up steep pitches as I watched in wonder, or poised on precipices with wind in their coats while surveying their wild domain.

The annual cycle of the mountain goat begins with the birth of offspring on winter ranges during late May and early June—a period that found me locating their kidding areas or camped on the cliffs to closely observe postpartum behavior. After a six-month gestation, a nanny will isolate herself from others and produce a single young, or rarely twins. Kids are born in particularly rugged, steep terrain, probably as an anti-predator strategy. From the moment of birth, their surroundings are vertical. This leaves a lasting impression of the way their environment should be oriented.

Newborn kids weigh just six to seven pounds, but are highly precocious. Barely an hour after its birth, I watched a kid struggle to follow its mother across a talus slope. On unsteady legs, he wobbled and tottered. His mother patiently waited each time the infant faltered and fell behind, sometimes returning to offer nudging encouragement. Being born into such surroundings means more than a few bumps on the chin, but predators are relatively few on the cliffs and nannies are doting mothers. When moving across steep inclines, nannies often position themselves just downslope of their kids, presumably to protect against miscues by their youngsters.

Newborns quickly gain strength. Within a week or two of birth, the spring migration to summer range begins as winter's grip weakens.

Fred Burr Creek near the author's winter camp in the Bitterroot Mountains—a fine place to take a refreshing sponge bath. (Photo by author)

An inquisitive kid goat in spring seeing who's come to call. (Photo by author)

Nannies often position themselves downslope on steep terrain, possibly to guard against any missteps by their rambunctious new charges. (Photo by author)

Kid goats are born to climb on anything, even their mothers. (Photo by author)

A camp on the cliffs during a week of observing
behavior of newborn goats in late May. (Photo by author)

Now nearly seven months old, Kam was big and strong enough to accompany me during a summer and fall in the high country. That's what I intended. But the wilderness has a way of swallowing up life. On our first trip in late June, he vanished while following me across a log that spanned a snowmelt-swollen torrent.

As swiftly as a misstep on ice-glazed granite or as an avalanche sweeps away a guiltless mountain goat, my wilderness companion was gone. My efforts failed to find him that day. Inquiries at local households and the animal shelter, and a newspaper ad could not bring him back. That summer was more solitary than I had expected, even when an occasional friend joined me on the summits. Only the goats and other wild alpine residents offered solace with any constancy. So I focused on that isolated assemblage of animals that persevere in near anonymity to those who live so far below.

I spent June to mid-October 1974 backpacking in 150 square-miles of high-country wilderness. The purpose was to follow the goats' wanderings which greatly expanded in summer across the Bitterroots' sprawling subalpine and alpine zones. For five to seven days each week I bounded the lengths of interfluvial ridges to the sky-scraping cirques and crests. These spiny ridges are united, like tines of a pitchfork, by the Bitterroot divide where Montana meets Idaho. Beyond to the west sprawled an immense jade sea of forest broken by rock and snow and nose-bleed crags. There, other goat herds wandered, as did some of the Bitterroot canyon animals I watched in winter.

Mountaineering agreed with me. Despite sixty-five pounds strapped on my back, rambling across talus and ragged ridges became as natural as breathing alpine air. As I learned the ropes of field research, I fancied the self-reliance that life in the wilderness demanded, without as much as a walkie-talkie for support (cell phones were not yet thought of). Where generations of sure-footed goats fattened and raised their kids, my bones might go undiscovered for decades.

Camped beside stately larch and ancient whitebark pines, snowmelt trickled past my tiny tent's door. A mantle of stars sometimes made me fight off sleep until immense fatigue prevailed. Surely this too was reward for the mountain goat, living at the roof of the world.

Some evenings I reconstituted freeze-dried meals on gaily flowered shorelines of Pearl, Totem, or dozens of other unnamed lakes. Those liquid gems pocked lofty basins, where silvery sentinels shimmered across their midnight waters. A twilight plunge into forty-degree depths left me refreshed, with fifteen hours of sweat scoured from skin and scalp. As onrushing storm clouds swallowed the failing alpenglow, I'd watch a nanny and kid or a stout billy nibble sprigs of St. John's wort en route to their sheltering, cliffside bedsites.

The author tagging the twigs of evergreen ceanothus (*Ceanothus velutinus*) shrubs in Fred Burr
Canyon in 1974 to measure their consumption by
mountain goats during winter. (Photo by author)

I've never felt more vulnerable and puny than when a storm bore down while I was
exposed near treeline and miles from anyone. The static electricity that prickled my skin
and twisted the hair on my arms into punk hairdos foretold the gathering electrons of a
close lightning strike. More than once I shed my camera and lenses, spotting scope and
tripod, and sprinted some distance away, only to see and hear a thunderbolt batter the
ridge nearby, leaving the acrid reek of splintered granite searing my eyes and nose. At
such moments I wondered if those same lightning strikes didn't occasionally clobber a
goat, though I've not read any reports of it. But then much about their lives remains
unknown to us. Such mysteries of nature are what draw inquisitive minds to the realm
of the mountain goat.

Summer is a time of plenty when meadows explode in vibrant color. On a banquet
of nutritious grasses, sedges, and forbs, goats recover from the previous winter, produce

milk to nurse young, and lay on fat for the coming winter. They focused like lasers on the new growth that's most readily converted to muscle and milk. In early summer this lush fare was ubiquitous, popping forth in the wake of melting snow. As the days shortened toward fall, prime foraging sites grew more sparse and spare and the goats traveled more.

Mostly from high vantage points, I found them and watched their activities. But occasionally, after cresting a ridge, they were far closer, offering a chance to record their feeding or snap a photograph. As I eavesdropped on mountain goats, other alpine fauna sometimes filled my spotting scope's field of view. Pikas, hoary marmots, and sometimes regal elk, plus American pipits and rosy finches constituted this hardy, high-living community. Twice I was treated to sightings of wolverines. One coursed with boundless energy through a confusion of boulders on a quest for a meal of marmots.

My closest encounters with mountain goats had been on steep winter range, where secure locations or energy conservation may have overcome their instincts to flee. Those meetings were also testament to these animals' trusting and curious nature. Sometimes they allowed me to slowly approach; other times I've had inquisitive animals check me out—even though these were hunted herds. One billy I met on a snow-slicked Bitterroot escarpment seemed way too interested. When he stiff-leggedly advanced to within about eight feet, then stomped a front foot, I folded my tripod and warily backed away.

But my closest encounter with a wild mountain goat was with the one that stepped on me. High in the Bitterroots in August I was scrambling across the ledgework skirting a picturesque cirque basin. Suddenly I spotted a nanny some one hundred yards off to my left. She was watching me from a shelf slightly lower than mine. I was at a spot where my ledge was some four or five feet wide, with drop-offs below and above, so I unshouldered my pack, set up my tripod and camera, and prepared to capture some photos of her. Just as I pressed my eye to the viewfinder, a kid goat bounded from my right and never slowed as it passed by. Much to my surprise, one hoof landed on my outstretched leg. Much to my disappointment, when I pulled up my pant leg the hoof had left no mark. Minutes later the kid was bumping its mother's belly for a drink of warm milk, but not before I'd snapped its picture shortly after the tyke had landed on me.

Summer fades in September. Needles of alpine larch change from lime to gold, then drop, leaving naked skeletal limbs until next May. As the grasses and wildflowers cure and store carbohydrates in root reserves, goats seek any remaining greenery where the nourishing moisture from remnant snowfields and seeps irrigate plants. Animals may still gain or at least not begin losing body weight by selecting the most nutrient-dense, digestible forage.

Even the goats that were hunted in Montana's Bitterroot Mountains could prove curious and trusting, as did this handsome billy. (Photo by author)

Billies range more widely in late October in search of females. The fall migration precedes or coincides with the November breeding season. Some goats followed the long ridges between drainages from the high country to cliffs 2,000 to 3,000 feet lower along the eastern half of canyons. Others descended to creek bottoms and crossed to the opposite south-facing canyon slopes—behavior registered by their tracks in fresh snow or from the electronic pathways I gleaned from radio collar signals. The first heavy snows that often precipitated the downward migration also flushed me from the heights back to the lower canyons—the winter asylum of the mountain goat.

The kid goat that stepped on the author during an August day in the Bitterroot Mountains. (Photo by author)

It would be satisfying to leave you with this blithe
image of North America's alpine athlete, or regale
you with more stories about the life it lives, the
feats it performs, or my own experiences among
the beasts. But as a scientist and conservationist,
there is more to the animal's story to tell. Across its
range, even the reclusive mountain goat shares its
prospects with others, including us, *Homo sapiens*,
the most numerous large mammal of all. Just as
yearling goats must coexist among bossy nannies, the
heavy hand with which we rule the land means that
mountain goats have faced, and will increasingly face,
challenges fitting into a human-dominated world.

So in the following chapters I explore our
influence on the animal and its wild realm. My
hope is that we learn from the past—what both
science and conscience instruct—and make
allowance for *Oreamnos americanus* tomorrow.

Part II

DOI: 10.5876_9781607322924.c006

Mountain goats are found in ten of the United States and four Canadian provinces and territories. To learn how many animals roam the continent, in 2011 I sent a questionnaire to wildlife managers in each of those fourteen jurisdictions. Based upon their responses and a 2011 report by the International Union for Conservation of Nature, the population totals roughly 100,000 mountain goats, making it one of the continent's least abundant hoofed animals.

The majority of goats roam coastal mountain ranges from Alaska to Washington. Smaller numbers dot the Rocky Mountain and Cascade chains and other, isolated mountain ranges. About half live in British Columbia and another quarter in Alaska.

During the late nineteenth and early twentieth centuries, many species of North America's large mammals suffered staggering population losses. Continental populations of elk, deer, pronghorn, bison, and most large carnivores were depleted by 90 percent and more. The mountain goat apparently was a fortunate exception. The protective advantage that goats had always enjoyed was that their wildland remoteness buffered them from human exploitation. Yet in recent decades many native herds declined in the southern part of the species' range. This transpired even as most ungulate

From the friendly confines of lush intermountain valleys, the mountain goat's realm may seem absent of life. The truth is, mountains support a diverse and vibrant community of plants and animals. (Photo by author)

Table 6.1. Estimated global population of ungulate species in North America in 2011

Species	Total Numbers
Mountain goat	100,000
Bighorn sheep	67,000
Dall and Stone sheep	115,000
Musk-ox	140,000
Moose	975,000
Elk	1,000,000
Pronghorn antelope	1,000,000
Caribou	4,000,000
Black-tailed and mule deer	7,000,000
White-tailed deer	26,000,000

Table 6.2. Recent numbers of mountain goats in each jurisdiction, population trends (S = stable, I = increasing, D = decreasing), and number of hunting permits issued in each state and province in 2011

State/Province	Estimated Population	Past 30-year Trend	Current Status	Permits
Alaska	24,000–33,500	S	S	Not limited
Colorado	1,680	I	S	209
Idaho	2,600	S*	S*	46
Montana	2,700	D	S**	285
Nevada	310	I	D	20
Oregon	850	I	I	13
South Dakota	80–100	D	S	2
Utah	2,000	I	I	111
Washington	2,400–3,184	D	D	20
Wyoming	350	I	S-I	24
Alberta	3,400	S	S	8
British Columbia	39,000–65,500	D	S-D	Not limited
Northwest Territories	2,000	Unknown	S	Not limited
Yukon Territory	1,700	Unknown	S	Not limited

* Transplanting programs to bolster or establish new herds have compensated for declines in some native herds.

** Native herds in western Montana are generally declining whereas introduced herds are stable or increasing.

numbers remained stable or increased in response to private and public conservation efforts. To understand the difference and the mountain goat's present conservation circumstances, let's look at what happened over the previous century.

It seems that improved access to goat ranges took a toll during the twentieth century. Logging and mining activities, recreational four-wheeling, and snowmobiling may have displaced animals to less suitable habitat or stressed animals during the environmentally most difficult season in a goat year. But the more pervasive threat was that better vehicle access made hunting easier. Many populations across southern Alberta and the Kootenay and Okanagan regions of British Columbia decreased in the 1960s to early 1970s. According to Canadian wildlife authorities, increased access combined with liberal hunting regulations produced "massive overharvest of populations." Similar scenarios occurred elsewhere in the Canadian and US Rockies but weren't fully realized until hunter success rates had dropped. The mountain goat may be the only North American ungulate to have suffered local extirpations through regulated hunting.

How large the loss of former goat numbers, no one really knows. In the mountain goat stronghold of British Columbia, for example, a government report states that 100,000 animals may have roamed the province in 1964. By 1977 the population was estimated at 63,000 and by 2011 somewhere between 39,000 and 65,500. Washington Department of Fish and Wildlife officials estimate that state's goat population has declined by two thirds over the past fifty years. The magnitude of declines in British Columbia, Washington, and elsewhere are approximations at best. Populations were not rigorously counted during the 1960s and before, and what survey data existed lacked a high degree of confidence. That a general decline occurred across most goat ranges, however, is acknowledged by wildlife authorities.

Contributing to this erosion of numbers was a poor understanding of the unique life history traits of the species, including: (1) the difficulty of distinguishing males from females; (2) low productivity of native goat populations; (3) the additive nature of hunting to other causes of mortality; (4) behavioral fidelity of goats to their habitat; and (5) the vulnerability of goats to harvest by humans compared to other hoofed mammals. Like its shaggy white cloak and rock climbing skills, the above suite of traits also defines America's rock goat, as we shall see.

Although they suit the palates of some hunters, mountain goats are not prized as table fare. Indeed in 1907, President Theodore Roosevelt, who hunted throughout the West, said he would not go after goats for meat because "the flesh usually affords poor eating, being musky." And on the heels of the collapse of most large-mammal populations in

Skulls from two adult goats I found in
Montana's Bitterroot Mountains: a male at
the top and a female below. (Photo by author)

the United States, William Hornaday of the New York Zoological Park wrote in 1914,
"This animal is not likely to be extirpated very soon," noting that they inhabit inaccessible
areas and the flesh is so musky and dry that it is not palatable.

While wildlife enthusiasts are struck by the beauty of mountain goats' regal pelage
and fascinating behaviors, it's the largest horns that entice most hunters. Yet, compared
to bighorn sheep, elk, deer, and moose, this animal sports diminutive headgear. Because
the average animal achieves 90 percent of its eventual horn length during the first three
years of life—about the time they become reproductively active—bragging rights separating the average four-year-old and nine-year-old, for example, are more or less aca-
demic and challenging to judge under hunting conditions.

Most jurisdictions allow either-sex hunting, in large part because goats have what
scientists refer to as limited sexual dimorphism. This means that the subtle differences
in physical appearance between the sexes (both are similarly colored, have beards, and
nearly identical horns) make it hard to separate males from females under field conditions. And because older males have higher winter mortality than their female counter-
parts, the sex ratio among adults becomes skewed toward females. Just by chance, with
more adult females in a population, hunters are more likely to harvest some nannies. As
a result, females typically comprise 20 to 40 percent of the harvest even when hunters
desire or are encouraged to shoot males.

Harvesting females can jeopardize the environmental resilience of a herd, and even its persistence. Females do not produce their first offspring until three to five years of age; they typically give birth to a single kid; and as much as a third of reproductively mature females do not bear young at all in a given year. Because of this low reproductive rate, *Oreamnos* replenishes lost herd members slowly, making each breeding-age nanny valuable to the herd. And because their reproductive success increases with age, females can make significant contributions to a population only by living long lives. After the age of about ten, birth rates among nannies start to decline. But those old-timers are no more likely to be chosen as trophies than prime breeding-age nannies (those five to nine years of age) because horn lengths (and therefore trophy appeal) increase little beyond three years of age. The similar appearance of the sexes and low reproductive rate are life history traits that warrant conservative harvest regulations.

Also at fault for falling goat numbers during the 1950s through the 1980s was the application of principles traditionally used to mange deer, elk, and other ungulates—species with greater productivity and less susceptibility to over-harvest. Because hunting mostly targets larger, adult goats, hunter take tends to be additive to natural mortality, which more often claims kids, yearlings, and the very old and feeble. In other words, hunting removes very few animals which were bound to die anyway from starvation, predation, accidents, or toothless old-age. The average age of the remains of twelve goats I found in the Bitterroots was 10.8, significantly older than the average age (6.0 years) of 123 goats harvested during those three years. The difficulty in distinguishing the age of goats three or more years old renders all adults, male and female, of similar trophy status to most hunters.

Furthermore, mountain goats are rigidly faithful to seasonal ranges, especially winter ranges. Because nursery groups return each fall to optimum areas of winter ranges, this is where numbers of goats are most visible and reliably found. In a long-term study in Idaho, Lonn Kuck found that as nannies were harvested from prime areas of the Pahsimeroi Range, some remaining goats from adjacent habitats moved in to occupy the preferred cliff areas. Billies are more solitary and may be harder for hunters to locate. As a consequence of these conditions, unsustainable harvests of females pare herds even though biologists and hunters continue to see similar numbers of goats in favored cliff habitats in the early stages of population declines.

Mountain goats are relatively easy to harvest with firearms. Seemingly secure on a pitch that only they can scale, or wisp of ledge from which to repel a wolf or lion's challenge, still leaves them vulnerable to a 200-yard (or longer) rifle shot. Certainly a hunter better have stout legs and lungs to hunt the mountain goat, but improved vehicle access has rendered some herds vulnerable to the lazy.

From the Cascade Mountains bordering Lake Chelan, a poignant example illustrates the acute vulnerability of the animal to modern transport and weapons. A story titled

Their handiwork endures more than 10,000 years later, where glaciers gouged U-shaped canyons in Canadian and US mountains. (Photo by author)

"Rare Sport on Cliffs" in the December 25, 1892, edition of the *New York Times* began: "They killed eleven goats—three billies, five nannies, and three kids. Their skins are on the steamer. They lost six goats that fell over the cliffs when they were shot." From pleasure ships and rowboats that plied Lake Chelan's waters, tourists and marksmen blasted away at white targets dotting cliffs above the shorelines of this fifty-five-mile-long gash into the heart of this Washington mountain goat stronghold. One historical report described the supply of goats as "inexhaustible." But like bison slayed from passenger trains, the carnage was unsustainable and slowed only when Washington established the first restrictions on goat hunting in 1897. Complete closure of all goat hunting in the state followed in 1925 and continued through 1947. Goat ranges bordering Lake Chelan were again closed to hunting in 1980. During the mid-1980s, forty-four goats were transplanted along the lake's shorelines to supplement the struggling population.

Even when modest harvest levels are intended, hunting pressure across many goat ranges can focus on certain groups of goats in a mountain range whereas other more remote groups escape much harvest. For example, wildlife managers may set a reasonable harvest quota of ten animals for an estimated population of 200 goats that roam a wide swathe of mountains. But much of the harvest may come from just fifty goats that use a section most accessible to hunters, draining that smaller area of animals in just a few years.

Finally, because they are less numerous and can withstand less hunting than more abundant and productive ungulates, wildlife management agencies have invested fewer resources in assessing the status of mountain goat populations. Most surveys to tally numbers are conducted in winter or early spring when goats are restricted to winter ranges. Surveys from the ground, like mine in the Bitterroots, afford the best opportunity to classify the age and sex of observed animals. But it's impractical to send a biologist or student scientist snowshoeing into every mountain hideaway where goats eke out a living. So, most assessments of goat herds are made from the birds-eye view of small aircraft, primarily helicopters. Due to costly air charter fees, few populations are surveyed annually—most only once every few years—and in the past, some not all.

So what do wildlife managers learn from these logistically difficult and costly surveys of mountain goats? Most basic is the number of animals presumed to occupy each survey area and the ages of animals observed. Based on studies in Alberta, Alaska, and Washington of their sightability (the percentage of animals observed of those actually there), 20 to 40 percent of goats in any one area are not spotted during survey flights (and maybe half in coastal forests of British Columbia and Alaska). Survey results must be adjusted accordingly to estimate total numbers. Counts from aircraft are generally limited to separating kids from older goats, so assessing herd sex ratios or survival of kids to yearling age is not possible.

All too common conditions that make surveying goats in winter challenging work. (Photo by author)

Clouds and fog often shroud the high elevations where mountain goats spend summer. Snow may be a visitor there any day of the year. (Photo by author)

Biologists use results of surveys repeated across several years to gauge population trends and set appropriate harvest levels. However, given the year-to-year variability of weather conditions, and the inherent inaccuracy and imprecision of survey results, wildlife managers have limited real-time knowledge of how populations are faring. This lack of reliable demographic data has historically produced belated adjustments in harvest quotas to shore up struggling herds. Because herds are slow to respond to relaxed hunting and seldom display compensatory growth (increased reproductive rate after herds are reduced, something that deer and elk herds may do where too many have formerly overused their food supply), goat numbers may languish at low levels. In some areas of Alberta, British Columbia, Idaho, Montana, and Washington, local populations have not recovered losses despite more than twenty years of closed hunting seasons. In such cases, other forms of ongoing human disturbance (such as seismic testing and helicopter overflights), habitat losses, and cumulative effects are believed to be the reasons for goat herds failing to rebound.

Following declines across their historical range, mountain goats were transplanted during the latter half of the twentieth century to bolster or to reestablish herds in Alaska, Idaho, Montana, Washington, Alberta, and British Columbia. The success rate of these restoration transplants has not always been stellar. Even when they've taken root, goats tend to multiply more slowly than reintroduced bighorn sheep, elk, or pronghorns.

During the warm Hypsithermal Period that followed retreat of the Pleistocene glaciers, fossil evidence suggests that goats likewise retreated, or died out, from areas south of their present native range. Due to their high fidelity to native ranges and fondness for rugged, remote places, goats didn't colonize isolated mountain "islands"—like the Absarokas, Beartooths, Snowcrests, and Tobacco Roots in Montana—even though such ranges may contain suitable habitat. To further expand recreational opportunities of this popular species—both for viewing and hunting—wildlife managers introduced mountain goats captured from native herds in Canada and the United States to these habitat islands and to six states south of their historical range.

Transplanted goats have readily adapted to their new homes from South Dakota to Oregon. Relatively mild climates, good range conditions, and few predators have fostered success of introductions outside historical range. Twenty-one released to Montana's Crazy Mountains in the 1940s increased to an observed population of 371 in 2011 while supporting sport hunting during most years. Other transplants enjoyed a period of rapid expansion, followed by a period of stabilization as animals fully occupied available habitat, followed by population decline as goats became limited by food resources,

Nannies seldom produce twins in native goat herds, but this one and her three-week-old offspring proved an exception. Lactating nannies are the last to shed their winter coats. In late June, this one is still weeks from completing the annual molt. (Photo by author)

disease, predators, or unknown factors. Such populations have since persisted at some post-decline level. The stagnation is typified by poor kid production and survival, but for reasons that are generally unclear.

Data from Idaho indicate that this sequence from transplant to post-decline may occur over thirty to forty years, as has been the case with goats transplanted in 1969 to the Palisades Wilderness Area of eastern Idaho. After at least twelve years of population increases of 20 percent annually (near the species' maximum reproductive potential), and sustained hunting and transplanting of surplus animals to other locations, numbers plummeted in the 1990s. Herd numbers remain very low despite sharp reductions in hunting and suspension of removals.

The Palisades area exemplifies the high reproductive potential of goats introduced to high quality habitats. Compared with native populations, nannies introduced to new ranges consistently first give birth at three years of age, have fewer reproductive pauses, and produce twins on occasion. What propels this early population growth is that most transplant sites are relatively predator-free, and competition for food and space is lax because bighorn sheep are absent. Introduced goats have flourished in Oregon's Hell's Canyon (of Evel Knievel motorcycle fame), where much of the canyon's habitat burned in 2007, possibly rejuvenating nutritious forage for the animals.

Studies suggest that introduced goats can be harvested at a much higher rate, up to 7 percent annually, without depressing numbers. If habitat is expansive or pathways are available to adjacent mountains, populations continue to expand in size as animals disperse and colonize additional range. Without traditional ties to their new surroundings, goats brought to Colorado and Utah have spread like molecules filling a vacuum.

But not all transplants have thrived, especially those in marginal mountain parcels such as the Gates of the Mountains Wilderness and the Elkhorn and Sapphire Mountains of Montana, and southern portions of British Columbia and Alberta's historic mountain goat range. Whether in native or transplanted populations, goats appear to fare worse in small, isolated areas where they have fewer places to relocate if habitat conditions worsen.

A few populations have done too well, some would argue, where they have grown and dispersed into adjacent areas where they may not be wanted. Mountain goats transplanted to Montana's Absaroka and Madison Ranges during the 1940s and 1950s began colonizing northern portions of Yellowstone National Park in the 1990s. Despite considerable harvest around the park's perimeter, more than 200 animals inhabited Yellowstone in 2011 with additional habitat still unoccupied, according to park biologists.

A handful of pioneers have spread as much as forty-four miles north into Grand Teton National Park from where goats were transplanted to Idaho's Palisades Wilderness two decades earlier. A lone apparition here, two or three clinging to a granite slab there are seen on occasion by mountaineers and rangers in the heart of what are called the

Wind-racked trees on a ridge bear witness to the brutal conditions
that the mountain goat endures. The lean of the dead trees evidences
the prevailing wind direction, as do the "flagged" trunks of the living
alpine larch (*Larix lyallii*) and subalpine firs (*Abies lasiocarpa*) whose
branches survive best on the leeward side of trunks. (Photo by author)

American Alps. Where they vanish in winter, no one knows. Likely they remain swallowed up on some wind-racked escarpment where even their tracks are erased from a
canvas the color of goats.

Sightings of nannies with newborns since 2008 suggest that a breeding population
has established in Grand Teton, as in nearby Yellowstone Park. This creates a dilemma for
National Park Service managers because America's mountain goat is not native to Grand
Teton and Yellowstone. Had colonizing goats originated from pioneering native populations, they would have been welcome. Instead, they are considered an exotic species—
not a natural component of the native biota. National Park Service policy prescribes that
when exotic plant and animal species find their way into parks: "Control or eradication
will be undertaken, where feasible, if exotic species threaten or alter natural ecosystems;
[or] seriously restrict, prey on, or compete with native populations." Management planning for Grand Teton's goats began in 2013.

A previous effort to manage goats in another US national park fueled years of
controversy and polarized public debate. A dozen animals introduced to Washington's
Olympic Mountains in the late 1920s preceded the establishment of Olympic National
Park in 1938. By 1983, an estimated 1,175 animals had colonized all suitable habitats on the
Olympic Peninsula, both within and around the park. By then, botanical studies showed

Beargrass (*Xerophyllum tenax*)—whose flower heads are relished by a variety of mammals—and Blodgett Mountain in the Selway-Bitterroot Wilderness Area. (Photo by author)

Like this one in Canada's Waterton Lakes National Park, bighorn sheep (*Ovis canadensis*) readily habituate to humans where they are not hunted, even learning the parking protocol in residential areas. (Photo by author)

that feeding and dust-bathing behavior of goats were damaging some species of rare, endemic plants. This prompted government officials to initiate a reduction program that removed 407 animals from the park from 1981 to 1989. Others were legally harvested beyond the park's borders leaving some 389 in the Olympic Mountains when the park's reduction program ended.

In recent years, Olympic National Park has managed goats under its "Hazard and Nuisance Animal Plan." The plan authorized hazing animals from certain popular tourist areas—goats hooked on tasty treats of an odd kind. As I described in Chapter 5, goats have a liking for salt—even an obsession that may make them confrontational. Behavior among Olympic's bad boys ranged from licking salty backpacks and hikers' clothes to their greatest weakness, lapping urine deposited where no outhouses are to be found. This became an unacceptable risk after a park tourist was fatally gored by an Olympic goat in 2011. Three other visitors were previously injured by habituated goats in the same area.

Given untold thousands of encounters between goats and people in the United States and Canadian parks, this human fatality in Olympic is a tragic anomaly. It pales compared to deaths from mountaineering mishaps, heart attacks, drownings, and even lightning strikes over the years. But a new planning effort began after a 2011 helicopter survey showed that goats were increasing again in Olympic National Park. It seeks to

Bighorn sheep in Alberta's Waterton Lakes National Park, possibly looking for a hidden spare key to the car's ignition? (Photo by author)

limit conflicts between mountain goats, people, and plants by capturing and transplanting some goats elsewhere.

This salt addiction is not unique to Olympic Park. Goats in Montana's Glacier National Park also shadow hikers at several popular areas of goat range. Look over your shoulder near Sperry Chalet or the Hidden Lake Overlook and a brazen billy or nanny may be following in your tracks. Despite their instinctual avoidance of people, wild animals in protected areas (and most often adult males) can become aggressive in their pursuit of salt. Just as unattended food and garbage can habituate bears, the tonic of human sweat and urine can encourage goats to lose their fear. Taking proper precautions or avoiding high risk places are choices that we, not the wildlife, can rationalize and choose to make.

To date, Olympic National Park is the only well-documented instance of goats adversely affecting an ecosystem. But not unlike Olympic, goats have accidentally colonized other national parks in the continental United States. In 1924, six animals were transported from Alberta to establish a herd in South Dakota's Custer State Park. Custer shares a common, fenced boundary with Mount Rushmore National Memorial, a unit of the National Park Service system. After arriving at Custer, several escaped their enclosure during their first night of confinement. Goats have since pioneered suitable habitat throughout the Black Hills, including scrambling with impunity beneath the chiseled stony stares of Washington, Jefferson, Roosevelt, and Lincoln. No control efforts

In some national parks, mountain goats have become habituated to humans, even traveling the pedestrian boardwalks at the Hidden Lake Overlook of Glacier National Park, Montana. (Photo by author)

followed, a wildlife official told me, because goat numbers have not exploded and damaged the national memorial's environment. A hit with tourists, as at other introduction sites, Rushmore's wooly residents rival the popularity of presidents.

Resource management decisions regarding exotic species, particularly one as charismatic and socially acceptable as the mountain goat, often involve a complicated blend of science, public opinion, societal values, and agency policy and law. But this can prove thorny maneuvering as in Colorado's case. The state's native bighorn numbers have undergone a decade-long slide, while introduced goats have dispersed far beyond introduction sites and pioneered habitats traditionally used by sheep. Meanwhile, managers of Rocky Mountain National Park worry that pioneering goats may displace or outcompete native bighorns. Since the 1990s park officials have removed each wayward goat that wandered into the park. The state of Colorado confronted this by declaring the goat a native species in 1993. The National Park Service disagrees. Based on an independent review of historical records, goats have not roamed Colorado in at least 200 years, not until their introduction from Montana in 1948. To date, the agencies have cooperated in these removals, a model that may someday be adopted in Wyoming's national parks.

Four presidents behold a nanny goat in
Mount Rushmore National Memorial.
(Chad Coppess, South Dakota Department of Tourism)

CHAPTER SEVEN

Conservation: Local Challenges

DOI: 10.5876_9781607322924.c007

Beyond the hazards of severe weather and gravity—environmental constraints by which the animal has been shaped through the diligent fine-tuning of natural selection—North America's mountain goat faces a host of new challenges. All of these are human-caused.

Beginning in the 1970s, concerns that many goat populations were dwindling spawned investigations of the species' ecology from Alaska to Montana. For the first time in 1976, agency scientists and student researchers gathered in Kalispell, Montana, to share their knowledge and concerns about the animal at the First International Mountain Goat Symposium. This began a tradition of convening a biennial meeting (the Northern Wild Sheep and Goat Council Symposium) to share research findings and report on the status of the mountain goat across its continental distribution. Thereafter, science began to play a greater role in the species' management.

It became clear that goats introduced to previously unoccupied habitats often underwent a boom and bust growth cycle, initially growing rapidly followed by population decline. To short-circuit anticipated declines, managers have sanctioned annual harvests of 7 to 10 percent by hunters to hold goat densities below range carrying capacity—an admittedly fuzzy metric. To

Out of nowhere. A two-year-old nanny in the Palisades Wilderness Area of Idaho. (Photo by author)

Like the nutrients of the plants they recycle, periodic wildfires have always been part of the mountain goat's ecology, making way for new plant growth in over-mature forests of the Rocky Mountains. On the contrary, tree canopies are essential for intercepting snow that permits goats to survive in Pacific coastal forests from Alaska to Washington. (Photo by author)

provide new herds for recreational hunting was of course the original purpose most transplants were conceived. The question lingers: would this boom and bust cycle occur uniformly for all newly established or reestablished populations? Apparently not, because some introductions have failed. Ten hunting districts in Montana, for example, closed to goat hunting between 1994 and 2008 due to declining goat populations. Seven of those districts had introduced populations. Where winters are more severe, or where habitat is limited or conducive to predation by wolves and grizzly bears, hunting may be unwarranted or may need to be far more conservative.

As if a different species, most native populations can withstand far less hunter removal than newly established herds. Across the species' range, hunting is regulated by issuing limited numbers of permits on a lottery basis, except in remote areas of Alaska, British Columbia, and Northwest Territories where hunting pressure is slight or unrestricted hunting accommodates First Nations' rights. Permit numbers and allocations are based on population trend data, which ideally would be collected annually. But gathering population data is constrained by budgets and logistics. So over the past decade managers have prescribed increasingly conservative harvests, largely as an upshot of past misjudgments that produced overharvests of goats.

The Montana wildlands where I lived among goats offers just one of many examples. The nineteen canyons of the northern Bitterroot Range comprise Hunting District 240. Following excessive harvest and decline of the population during the twentieth century, hunting in 240 was closed from 1948 to 1954. After hunting reopened in 1955, Montana issued seventy-five or more permits each year during the 1960s and 1970s producing annual harvests averaging thirty-seven animals—more than 10 percent of the district's estimated population of 300 goats. My observations during the mid-1970s suggested that losses from natural causes doubled that annual mortality rate. Even if every adult female had produced and successfully raised a kid each year, that would not have offset total annual losses. In response to plummeting goat numbers and productivity, in 2011 only twelve permits were offered for Hunting District 240 and only two permits in 2012.

Over the past thirty years, wildlife officials have pared back hunting of native populations in most provinces and states. In the Bob Marshal and Great Bear Wilderness Areas, two other Montana strongholds of native goats, populations have shrunk by an estimated 85 percent in recent years and hunting has all but ended. The number of permits to hunt goats in Idaho's Pahsimeroi Mountains, where biologist Lonn Kuck documented how excessive harvests had sent that population into a tailspin, was slashed from twenty to forty annually during the 1970s to four permits in 2012. And in 1988, Alberta halted hunting of dwindling mountain goats province-wide. As populations slowly recovered in subsequent years, very conservative hunting was reinstituted in 2001 for this highly popular big game species.

Encouragingly, this conservative pattern demonstrates agencies responding to better data and our emerging understanding of mountain goat biology. It's an acknowledgment that herds can withstand little hunter harvest on top of natural mortality. I'm hopeful that greater recognition of the animal's nonconsumptive values has also compelled tighter harvest measures.

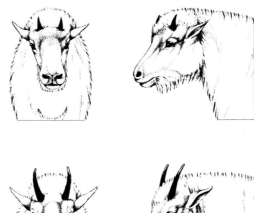

Frontal and lateral views of kid (above) and yearling mountain goats. (From Smith 1988, *Journal of Mammalogy*)

Regulations nowadays generally limit annual harvests to 1 to 4 percent of native populations and recognize the particularly vulnerable nature of isolated, small herds. In Alberta, Alaska, British Columbia, Idaho, and Oregon, populations numbering less than fifty individuals are generally not hunted at all. Washington State recently increased the minimum population size that can be hunted from fifty to one hundred. In many jurisdictions large hunting units have been subdivided to apportion hunting permits in accordance with judged vulnerability of individual herds. Management is catching up with the science. The mountain goat's ecology, socio-biology, and population dynamics are unlike any other North American big game animal—truths that must inform its conservation.

Maybe more than any other factor, the revelation that breeding age females of this matriarchal species should be exempted from harvest has been a vital contribution of recent field studies. In most jurisdictions, harvest of females is discouraged yet not prohibited. Poor sexual dimorphism of the species—the sexes' near mirror image—has kept wildlife managers from requiring harvest of only males.

To foster protection of females, I published a paper in 1988. It illustrated in words and drawings the field markings that are useful to discriminate males from females, as well as four age classes of mountain goats. Such educational materials have increasingly been provided to hunters in pamphlets and identification quizzes to curb the shooting of females.

Sport hunting of goats is acceptable because it provides recreational opportunities for hunters and economic benefits for hunting guides. And hunters have traditionally been financial stalwarts in support of wildlife conservation. Yet continental participation in recreational hunting continues its decades-long slide. According to the 2011 National Survey of Fishing, Hunting, and Wildlife-Associated Recreation, only 11.6 million

Frontal and lateral views of two-year-old female (above) and adult female mountain goats. (From Smith 1988 *Journal of Mammalogy*)

Frontal and lateral views of two-year-old male (above) and adult male mountain goats. (From Smith 1988, *Journal of Mammalogy*)

Americans hunted big game out of 90 million Americans aged sixteen and older who participated in recreational activities related to fish and wildlife.

Unlike many populations of ungulates—and especially those that are relatively predator-free—goats do not "require" sport hunting to limit their numbers and consequent conflicts with humans and agriculture. On the contrary, native populations do just fine if they are not hunted by us. As evidence of this, numbers have remained relatively stable in national parks of the United States and Canada.

This leads to the reality that this North American novelty's value increasingly lies in nonconsumptive uses, such as wildlife observation, nature study, and photography. As permits for hunting goats become increasingly rare, the allure of the species has never been higher. In Canada's Banff, Glacier, Jasper, Kluane, Kootenay, Nahanni, Revelstoke, Waterton, and Yoho parks, spotting goats clinging to cliffs is as much a part of the visitor's experience as ogling the stunning scenery that the goats roam. The animal most closely associated with Montana's Glacier National Park is the mountain goat. Over two million tourists annually seek a chance to spot and photograph the animal rambling the park's Pleistocene ice-sculpted ramparts. In Washington's North Cascades National Park—where I surveyed populations as a seasonal employee in 1976—glimpsing this shaggy mountaineer also delights tourists. The area in and around Klondike Gold Rush National Park and the town of Skagway, Alaska, draws about 800,000 tourists annually,

Welcome goat at the Izaak Walton Inn, Essex, MT. (Photo by author)

GLACIER PARK, INC. TRANSPORTATION

Emblem on door of Glacier National Park's concessionaire Red Bus tour vehicles. (Photo by author)

GREAT NORTHERN RAILWAY

X 97   YOUR *SAFETY* IS UP TO *YOU*   RADIO EQUIPPED   X 97

Logo on Great Northern railroad cars. (Photo by author)

Mountain Goat road sign. (Photo by author)

MOUNTAIN GOATS

OVERHEAD

with viewing of glaciers and goats the primary draw. And in Colorado and Oregon, outdoor clubs devoted to the mountain goat and their alpine habitat are thriving.

In a 2011 survey I asked wildlife biologists and managers across the fourteen states, provinces, and territories inhabited by mountain goats to list the most urgent conservation and management needs of the species. The list included more funding for research and for population surveys, but most often mentioned were measures to protect herds from both habitat and population impacts.

Although the realm of the mountain goat remains relatively unchanged, no other large mammal may be as sensitive to modification of its habitat as this one. The species is a habitat specialist. If its habitat is safeguarded from human incursions, it does well where populations are protected from over-exploitation. Our enterprises that directly degrade and fragment its domain include mining, logging, energy exploration and development, and recreational ventures.

Harvesting timber from coastal mountain goat ranges may be the most significant habitat threat. By intercepting winter snows and nurturing arboreal lichens that goats eat, ancient trees enable goats to survive beneath their crowns. Without the "umbrella" provided by these old-growth tree canopies, goats that have prospered in coastal ranges for generations could literally be buried beneath maritime snows. "Because goat winter habitat is limited," concluded a 1989 study by the US Forest Service of declining populations in Alaska, "even small areas of habitat alteration that impinge on these areas can have a disproportionately large effect on the goat populations concentrated there."

Beyond degrading areas of habitat, the roads that accompany industrial and recreational activities bring more people into goat ranges. That makes hunting and viewing easier, but associated disturbance also affects goats in ways we are only beginning to understand. Physiological stress (which can depress immune system function and burn energy reserves), separation of nannies and kids, and displacement from preferred areas—especially winter habitats—can threaten the survival of individual animals and the vitality of herds. Montana goat biologist Gayle Joslin described such a situation along Montana's Rocky Mountain Front where seismic exploration activity was ostensibly responsible for mountain goat population declines.

> At some unknown but relatively minor level, human disturbance in mountain goat habitat results in declining goat populations. This has been repeatedly displayed across North American goat country . . . Although not much research has been done on the effects of stress on goat physiology, researchers have studied it extensively

One of the Bitterroot canyons where road-building and logging (cut blocks near the ridge top) occurred above winter cliffs (lower left) used by mountain goats. (Photo by author)

in mountain sheep and other wildlife. Research from Alberta shows that even if an animal does not respond outwardly to disturbance, it does not necessarily mean an animal is not responding internally through increased adrenalin output, raised heart rate, or other reactions. Research also shows that if stress is repeated or prolonged, resistance to infection and disease may decrease and reproduction may be impaired or completely fail.

Another concern is the upsurge in off-road vehicles and high-powered snowmobiles penetrating mountain goat ranges. As snow settles and compacts in late winter, snow-mobilers like to "high-mark" on mountainsides, sometimes encroaching on goat habitat. Then snowmobiling can elevate animals' stress and calories spent at a time when winter-weary and pregnant goats can least afford it.

In addition to these conservation challenges, when I asked wildlife managers about future threats to goats, those most often mentioned were recreational and industrial harassment from motorized equipment, especially helicopter overflights. Although goats may respond to low-flying airplanes, it's the sound of approaching helicopters that send these cliff-dwellers into a panic. After four years of extensive oil and gas exploration along Montana's Rocky Mountain Front, that goat population had fallen by 35 percent,

In the crystalline hush of winter, a mountain goat's breath lingers. (Photo by author)

largely due to a dramatic drop in kid production and survival. Gayle Joslin attributed the decline to hundreds of helicopter overflights for seismic testing.

Goats and helicopters mix like water and oil. Throughout their range, they react frantically to approaching whirlybirds. We don't know if goats perceive the thundering approach of a Jet Ranger as some gargantuan eagle, an airborne avalanche, or some other dire threat to their lives. Watching them scurry to hunker against cliff walls or tremble beneath trees, their reactions are unmistakably fearful.

We can't even be sure which disturbances affect goat survival or reproduction most. Or specifically how metabolic pathways are compromised. Our best scientific efforts surely would pale in comparison to the reclusive mountaineer just telling us the answers to such matters. Studies of more amenable research subjects inform us that combinations of offenses invariably inflict more harm than they do individually, something scientists call "cumulative effects." The population declines Gayle Joslin recorded were more evident in an area with a long history of human-related activities, many involving year-long mechanized access. After seismic activity abated in 1985, the goat population in this area of human disturbance recovered much more slowly than in an adjacent, relatively pristine area without motorized access, suggesting disturbances cumulatively diminished the vitality of goat herds.

But helicopter use in goat habitat is not solely a result of energy exploration and development. Recreational flights into goat ranges of Alaska, British Columbia, Yukon Territory, Idaho, Washington, and Wyoming are a booming industry that encompasses flight-seeing tours and transport for heli-skiing and heli-hiking. This explosion of helicopter-based recreation suggests to me that heli-barbeques and heli-weddings (with goats as invited guests) are an untapped market for those who can pay. Such airborne intrusions are ironically self-defeating, degrading the solitude we seek in backcountry retreats. More to the point, they are a menace to the reclusive mountain goat, particularly during winter and early kid-rearing months. Helicopter disturbance has been compared to an increase in predation risk. It alters physiological condition, depresses reproductive success, and even risks injuries to fleeing animals. Canadian research indicates that mountain goats fail to habituate to helicopter overflights that continue over years.

A growing body of evidence of these negative effects prompted wildlife scientists to write a position statement on the subject in 2004. Released by the Northern Wild Sheep and Goat Council, the statement recommends restrictions on the timing and proximity of helicopter overflights in goat ranges. Each mountain goat is an individual. All do not respond the same to helicopters, or for that matter to other stimuli in their environment. But the pattern is clear.

Although we all use wood products, minerals, and fossil fuel energy to enrich our lives, we can temper our choices. People can make informed decisions about how and

The mountain goat faces many conservation challenges. Among them is the spread of invasive plant species such as the common mullein (*Verbascum thapsus*) that's multiplying across parts of Montana's Glacier National Park. (Photo by author)

Jones' columbine (*Aquilegia jonesii*) is one of many native alpine flowers that grace the mountain goat's summer range. (Photo by author)

A wildlife underpass incorporated into highway construction to accommodate movement patterns and limit vehicle collisions with mountain goats. (Photo by author)

where and to what extent we alter our environment; and how we impact other life forms with lifestyles far less flexible than our own. Given the precarious nature of its life lived on the edge, the mountain goat is deserving of our benevolence.

For all the security and calm its chosen haunts would seem to offer, each year less remains untouched by our pursuit of more resources and new playgrounds. I can make the case that lands where wolverines, hoary marmots, and mountain goats breathe and

Goats spend vast amounts of time looking over the edge of their world. (Photo by author)

A sign advising recreationists they are entering a restricted travel zone within Idaho's Sawtooth National Recreation Area. The restrictions are designed to reduce stress and displacement of wintering mountain goats. (Sawtooth National Recreation Area Archives)

breed most clearly define a mountain wilderness. Indeed, the single most effective conservation policy for sustaining goat herds may be formal designation of wilderness, or at least forbidding motorized travel in mountain goat range. Such a ban on heli-skiing in portions of Idaho's Sawtooth National Recreation Area was instituted in the 1970s and subsequently expanded to protect wintering mountain goats. In 2002, federal land managers in coordination with the Idaho Fish and Game Department enacted voluntary winter closures on snowmobiling, skiing, and other recreational uses in areas where goats were subject to disturbance. Seasonal closures such as these may provide goats the margin of security needed to persist in areas formerly frequented only rarely by people. In the dead of winter, goats have nowhere else to go; people do.

DOI: 10.5876_9781607322924.c008

CHAPTER EIGHT

The Global Challenge

Even as some threats to species may be regulated and ameliorated at the local level, others cannot. A growing global challenge now confronts alpine environments and their wild residents, including the mountain goat.

The evidence is undeniable that our planet is warming, atmospheric accumulation of greenhouse gases is largely responsible, and Earth's ecosystems and biodiversity are already suffering the effects. These realities are well-documented in countless scientific publications and summarized in comprehensive reports of the Intergovernmental Panel on Climate Change (IPCC). The IPCC was established in 1988 by the United Nations to assess current scientific, technical, and socio-economic information worldwide about the risk of climate change caused by human activity, its potential environmental and socio-economic consequences, and options for human adaptation to these climate-caused effects. Thousands of experts in climate science and related fields from 120 countries contribute to the panel's assessments.

Although some consequences of the planet's warming may bring welcome changes on local scales—most notably for those who aren't fans of parkas and mukluks—negative consequences will predominate. For example, warmer and longer growing seasons and the fertilization effect of rising CO_2 levels will accelerate growth rate of plants, potentially boosting crop yields and increased consumption of CO_2 (a major greenhouse gas and fuel for photosynthesis). However these benefits will be offset by increasingly variable precipitation patterns, withering heat and drought, geographical shifts in food production zones, and plagues of agricultural pests.

Our warming climate is impacting biota from the poles to the equator. But it's at the highest latitudes and altitudes that the changes are most dramatic. Annual temperatures of polar regions and the arctic alpine are climbing at triple the rate of other regions of the globe. Conditions have always been most frigid at these geographic extremes, and by definition their life forms are cold-adapted.

The whitebark pine is one such species adapted to ice-box temperatures and blistering winds that shape the upper treeline across much of the mountain goat's interior range. Yet from Colorado to British Columbia the tree is dying. In the Greater Yellowstone Ecosystem, almost half of whitebark pines are now dead. More broadly, vast tracts of Rocky Mountain spruce and pine forests have become eerie landscapes of arboreal skeletons after dying orange needles fall from gray, lifeless limbs. Their ongoing demise has been traced to increased pine blister rust and mountain pine beetles formerly held in check by the winter deep freeze. Temperatures are no longer cold enough long enough to beat back the pests that attack and kill trees that are increasingly weakened by warm, dry summers. Dead forests become tinderboxes for wildfires that have been raging across western wildlands as the wildfire season has lengthened by weeks. Such effects not only destroy commercial forests, they accelerate the addition of CO_2 to the atmosphere and change ecosystems in numerous ways and more rapidly than many species can adapt.

It's a big deal to the Clark's nutcracker, which makes a steady diet of the whitebark's pine nuts, and also to threatened grizzly bear populations in Wyoming, Montana, and Idaho who relish the cones as a high-energy, pre-denning food source. The bears get them not by climbing trees, but by raiding winter food caches diligently stored by red squirrels. Additional reverberations ripple throughout the alpine zone's web of life from the loss of this single species of tree.

Warmer conditions are expected to advance phenological events such as flowering and fruiting of plants demanding species dependent on them to reset migration timing, breeding, and other biological cycles. The transformation is altering distributions of whole plant communities, changes scientists have been measuring on the ground and with the aid of satellite imagery in recent years. Trends over the past three or four decades show an accelerating expansion of species' geographic range boundaries toward the poles or to higher elevations by progressive development of new local populations. Concurrently, opportunistic, weedy, or highly mobile species are invading new

The Clark's nutcracker's (*Nucifraga columbiana*)
long and powerful beak is adept at prying the
high-energy seeds from whitebark pine cones.
(Courtesy Shana S. Weber)

(*overleaf*) Dying whitebark pine (*Pinus albicaulis*) has
become a common sight in the subalpine zone of
the mountain goat's range as unchecked disease and
parasites attack heat-stressed trees. (Photo by author)

areas, especially where native species are declining. Ecosystems will gain some species and lose others with consequent reorganization of community relationships and food webs.

The Earth has warmed before, but it's the rate of temperature rise that worries observers. In many regions the climate threat promises to overtake habitat loss and fragmentation, pollution, human exploitation, and the spread of invasive species and disease as the preeminent threat to biodiversity. As the warming continues more species will be put to the test: can they adapt as rapidly as the changing weather?

Given this bleak picture of an over-heating planet, what might the future hold for America's shaggy alpinist and his mountain stronghold? A look at the past may help. During the Hypsithermal—a 6,000-year post-Pleistocene stretch when temperatures averaged some four degrees Fahrenheit warmer than the present—mountain goat populations died out south of Idaho, Montana, and Washington. Glaciers in the Cascades and Rockies melted, treeline marched up mountainsides, and alpine species receded northward. These same changes in ice and species' distributions are now being repeated, at a much accelerated pace, as the size of the alpine zone effectively shrinks.

According to the IPCC's 2007 report, climate-change models suggest an average two-degree Fahrenheit increase in global mean temperature over the next fifty years. The change will be far greater near the poles and at high elevations. Such warming is predicted to force a shift of ecosystems nearly 1,000 feet higher in elevation and 100 miles farther north. The IPCC also forecasts that more than 50 percent of the alpine-tundra ecosystems will eventually disappear as forests advance up mountains.

Most of us know from media reports that from the Himalayas to the Alps, and the Andes to the Rockies, continental glaciers are in retreat. These iconic features of the mountain goat's domain are destined to become relics and then memories of the Earth's former, cooler past—a bleak bellwether of the heating's effects.

From a total count of 150 in 1850, Montana's famous glaciers in Glacier National Park had shrunk to 25 in 2013. Scientists predict all will have melted away between 2020 and 2030. Glacier will become un-Glacier or formerly Glacier National Park, and the trend is similar throughout the mountain goat's range. The downstream effects will include diminished water flows in summer and fall, jeopardizing water-dependent wildlife, like Glacier's native cutthroat trout.

The full impact of glacial retreat on Glacier Park's mountain ecosystem is not fully known, but at least one aquatic species already faces extinction. As its name implies, the meltwater stonefly (*Lednia tumana*) prefers the coldest, most sensitive alpine stream

Glacier, 1911
Elrod photo, K. Ross Toole Archives, U of M

(*above*) Jackson Glacier 1911. **(US Geological Survey)**

(*below*) Jackson Glacier 2009. **(US Geological Survey)**

(*above*) Shepard Glacier 1913. (US Geological Survey)

(*below*) Shepard Glacier 2005. (US Geological Survey)

A meltwater stonefly (*Lednia tumana*)
photographed in Glacier National Park
in 2010. (Courtesy Joe Giersch)

habitats directly downstream of disappearing glaciers, permanent snowfields, and springs in the park. Recorded only from Glacier National Park and nearby areas, and with a distribution so dependent on frigid waters, concerned scientists sought protection of the meltwater stonefly as an endangered species. In 2011, the US Fish and Wildlife Service ruled the insect warrants protection under the Endangered Species Act. However, the fate of higher priority plants and animals (those at greater risk of extinction) needed attention first; so the stonefly joined 259 other species on a waiting list. While awaiting consideration for listing, these candidate species receive no statutory protection.

Loss of the meltwater stonefly may seem inconsequential: a bug in the water that most of us have never and will never see. But it's not alone in its icewater environment. "The real take-home message is that we really aren't just dealing with one single species here. We're dealing with a whole ecosystem of interest: a very rare ecosystem that is dependent on very cold and permanent water," notes Joe Giersch. An aquatic entomologist at the US Geological Survey, Giersch has been studying Glacier Park's isolated alpine streams for fifteen years and found additional species that appear endemic there as well. These aquatic invertebrates are predicted to lose 80 percent of their habitat as glaciers melt and snowpack recedes.

In their own way, goats rely on this water too. Although future precipitation patterns are sketchier to predict than the trajectory of the temperature, warming and shortening winters will see more precipitation as rain than snow. Fading glaciers and snowfields will shrivel dependable water sources for growing the most nutritious plants. Recent research by biologist Kevin White and his colleagues showed that two environmental factors dominated survival of Alaskan mountain goats. Total snowfall in winter exerted the strongest effect. As described in this book's earlier chapters, food scarcity and the physical challenges of living in deep snow test wintering goats across most of their geographic range.

Of secondary importance, White found that summer temperatures indirectly influence survival during the following winter. And this is where alpine meltwaters come in. Cool summers prolong emergence of herbaceous plants at the edge of slowly receding snowlines. Early phenological growth stages of plants are less lignified, meaning they're more digestible and therefore promote higher weight gains in animals. Recent research on the mountain goat's relative, the European chamois, found that weights of yearlings were strongly related to growing season temperatures. Over sixteen years of study, yearling weights declined as spring and summer temperatures increased. Just as cool summers prolong diet quality of Alaskan goats—boosting weight gains and fat for winter living, which enhance survival—slow-release meltwaters from the receding snowpack irrigate the lush grazing gardens of the chamois and the goat. And in a species whose young are already disadvantaged by small size in winter, good summer nutrition is important for milk production and growth of kid goats. The good news is that given their generalist diet, mountain goats will likely fare better than feeding specialists that share their warming environment.

Then again, goats show intolerance to summer heat, often bedding in shade and on or near residual snow. Idaho wildlife biologist Dale Toweill expresses concern for the mountain goat's future in a state where little alpine habitat already exists, and some populations occupy suitably rugged habitat at lower elevations—as they do in South Dakota and parts of Oregon. It's probably no accident that at the southern extreme of its

Monkey flower (*Mimulus lewisii*) is one of the many lovely flowering plants that grace mountain goat habitats. This one is found along small streams and springs fed by the dependable meltwaters from snowfields and glaciers. (Photo by author)

A nanny is a doting mother
throughout the first year of her
offspring's life. (Photo by author)

present distribution, Colorado's introduced animals roam the highest elevations of any living mountain goats. Were Colorado's peaks 3,000 to 4,000 feet lower, as in Idaho and Montana, could the shaggy beast persist in our rapidly warming world?

Gazing at distant peaks, some might conclude that such bleak and barren blocks of rock are lifeless or at least support no life of consequence. Yet, a tenacious assemblage of cold-adapted biota eke out an existence where summers are measured as mere bursts of vitality sandwiched between the ends and beginnings of a crystalline hush.

One alpine neighbor of the mountain goat may serve as a biological indicator of the rising heat. The American pika, also known as the rock rabbit or cony, is North America's diminutive relative of the rabbits and hares. This quarter-pound hoarder survives six-month winters feasting on haystacks of vegetation that she cuts and stores under boulders blanketing subalpine and alpine slopes. As long as she isn't a slacker and stockpiles enough fodder, she feasts comfortably beneath an insulating quilt of snow.

Although the densely furred pika is sensitive to warm summer temperatures, she behaviorally compensates. As the days heat up she avoids thermal stress by retreating to cooler microclimates beneath boulders and talus. But as alpine temperatures have risen some four degrees over the past fifty years, it's the associated changing pattern of precipitation that concerns most pika biologists. As declining snowfall fails to accumulate to depths that insulate their subnivean sanctuaries, pikas may fare poorly during the winter months—and most notably at lower altitudes where winter snowpack is often most skimpy. Some low elevation populations of pikas inhabiting Great Basin mountain ranges of Nevada and Oregon have vanished in the past century, whereas those surveyed at higher elevations are generally doing well. Ironically, global warming might unduly subject pikas to cold temperature stress as their protective winter blanket wears thin in a warming world.

The animal whose geographic range most closely overlaps the mountain goat's has chosen a different lifestyle than the pika. While eating all that she harvests from May to September, the hoary marmot impersonates Rip Van Winkle burrowed beneath boulders and snow for the rest of the year. She amasses belly rolls of fat to fuel her long hibernation demands. If all goes well, she'll emerge with adequate reserves to breed and raise a litter during the short season of renewal.

Studies in Colorado of the closely related yellow-bellied marmot show that hibernation duration has shortened and marmots are growing bigger—both observations attributed to warming. The more northerly distributed hoary marmots, besides having a thick coat of dark fur that readily absorbs solar energy and restricts heat loss, have no sweat glands and cannot pant to dissipate body heat. As a result, their body temperature increases with the external air temperature. Add to this the insulation of accumulating body fat and it is obvious that hot summer days do the marmot no favor. To escape such weather, hoary marmots take refuge underground—sometimes for days—which counters the foraging advantages of lengthening growing seasons.

Hibernating in deep winter burrows, marmots may prove more physiologically tolerant of the changing alpine climate than the pika, yet still be tested in other ways. As high elevations warm and dry, the nutritious foods they require may become scarce as summers lengthen, and meltwaters run out earlier. Successful marmots may focus on shrinking green meadows, thus putting competitive pressure on populations.

The carnivorous counterpart of the mountain goat—at least in grit and geographic distribution—is the wolverine. Besides thirty pounds of boundless audacity, the wolverine's specializations—thick coat, huge feet, and fearless attitude—enable it to endure the frigid months of America's wildest wildlands, much like the mountain goat. And like the goat, its historic range spanned the northern Rockies and Cascades, but unregulated killing by humans during the twentieth century eliminated wolverines from much of their southern distribution. In response to more conservative trapping regulations, perhaps 300 wolverines now share the contiguous US range of the mountain goat.

Contrary to the goat's sedentary winter lifestyle, wolverines are high-energy carnivores. They seem to relish covering immense tracks of terrain to find the next meal in a landscape that's starkly devoid of life half the year. Goats seem bound to summer snow for thermoregulation and its meltwater irrigation of lush vegetation, whereas wolverines depend on deep snowpack that persists into May. Females produce two or three kits in late winter in elaborate natal dens they excavate five or more feet deep in stable snow. In these high mountain nurseries, mothers nurture their young for several weeks, sheltered from the outside cold and would-be predators.

Persistent snow is an invariant necessity of their environment for reproduction and for caching and preserving food for leaner times. On top of other threats to their conservation, the warming climate compelled conservationists to petition the US Fish and Wildlife Service to protect the wolverine under the Endangered Species Act. Just as it seemed the pika might be the first mammalian casualty of climate change to be listed as federally threatened—and the meltwater stonefly the first invertebrate—the wolverine was relegated in 2010 to the list of candidate species. Although agreeing that the wolverine warranted Endangered Species Act protection in the contiguous United States, the agency concluded that it was of lesser risk of extinction than other candidate species demanding the agency's limited resources for rulemaking and recovery plan implementation. Then, in compliance with a litigation settlement, in January 2013 the agency proposed Endangered Species Act protection for the wolverine in the lower forty-eight states. A final ruling is expected in early 2014. But if listed as a threatened species, federal officials

At just three to four ounces, the pika (*Ochotona princeps*) is barely palm-sized, yet survives bone-chilling, six-month winters beneath an insulating blanket of snow dining on vegetation it harvested and stacked in piles during summer. (Courtesy Jim Jacobson © 2011)

The range of the wolverine (*Gulo gulo*) closely overlaps the mountain goat's. Both share cold weather adaptations that enable them to thrive in the mountains of western North America. **(Photo from Wikimedia Commons)**

made clear they won't use the animal's status as a means to regulate greenhouse gases blamed for accelerating climate change. The George W. Bush administration placed a similar caveat on the conditions of listing the polar bear as a threatened species in 2008.

So much about the future of these and other alpine species is uncertain, completely uncharted biological territory. Answers are elusive about how the planet's warming will affect plants and animals and, indeed, we likely don't know all the relevant questions to ask. Some species, like the ermine, snowshoe hare, and white-tailed ptarmigan, rely on cryptic coloration to enhance their hunting prowess or as defense against becoming prey. Each replaces its summer fur or feathers in fall with a camouflaged dress of winter white. As winters shorten, can these species' biological calendars reset successfully to delay morphing to white in autumn and yet accelerate molting to summer attire earlier in spring? How many other species face similar conundrums, constrained by the rate at which their bodies and behavior can adapt?

It's unclear if the moderating climate may increase predation risk should goats spend more time in forested habitat. Or might changes in parasite loads, life cycles, and their

Perfectly camouflaged on a mottled background of snow and rock, the white-tailed ptarmigan (*Lagopus leucura*) changes from white in winter to a mostly brown plumage in summer. (Glacier National Park archives)

transmission vectors bode poorly for the mountain goat? As in the case of the marmot, a warming environment may effectively contract the size of the goat's late summer-fall habitat. With an upward shift in treeline, mountain goats may move to higher elevations, effectively sequestered on shrinking islands in the sky.

Altered habitats, in combination with other troubles discussed in the previous chapter, could conspire to pare numbers and predispose herds to small population effects. Many transplanted populations began with only ten to fifteen founder animals, and many isolated native herds number less than fifty individuals. Tiny populations are at greater risk of unusual mortality events, but also inbreeding depression stemming from limited genetic variation—already a genetic trademark of *Oreamnos* based on recent molecular studies. In this species bound to steep country and not prone to dispersing, these cumulative effects could diminish viability of populations.

While managing harvest and human disturbance requires herd-specific plans, conservation of mountain goats must also include a broader, landscape approach. To accommodate outbreeding via the random dispersing of individuals, we must conserve connecting

Another mammal of the subalpine and alpine zones, the golden-mantled ground squirrel (*Spermophilus lateralis*) is twice the size of a chipmunk. Like the hoary marmot, it hibernates during winter. **(Photo by author)**

routes between potentially isolated "population islands." But ultimately, remedying climate change and other threats to alpine species requires constraining human resource consumption, especially the burning of fossil fuels. Although our species is adaptable and we may muddle our way through if we fail to reverse the climate trend, we will find a planet impoverished of life forms a more demanding and less vibrant place to live.

Despite the challenges to its wellbeing, the mountain goat thrills wildlife enthusiasts across its US and Canadian range. I count myself among the fortunate who have spent memorable days among these shaggy mountaineers. One August morning in Montana's Bitterroot Mountains captured the wonder of the animal's lofty realm. Beyond my perch dividing two glacier-gouged canyons, a broad cirque basin sprawled in the yawning shadow of two majestic peaks. Through binoculars and tripod-mounted spotting scope,

The gray-crowned rosy finch (*Leucosticte tephrocotis*)
can be found feeding on and near alpine snowfields
and nesting in crevices of cliffs. (Photo by author)

I scanned sweeps of granite, flowered gardens, and melting snowdrifts for the Old Man
of the Mountains. Rewarding my squinting, a display of wildlife burst from that grand
mosaic.

"Eeeeek," a pika announced her presence from a sunny balcony, then returned to
stockpiling hay for the upcoming winter. Grey-crowned rosy finches flicked in and out
of cracks in cliffs where they may have raised another year's brood of chicks. A half
mile distant, a dark object caught my eye. Popping like a periscope from a jumble of
boulders, a wolverine came bounding my way. Like a game of hide and seek, he would
navigate hidden pathways then reappear ever closer to appraise his intended prey. One of
the hoary marmots spotted the would-be assassin. He whistled a high-pitched alarm to
his less vigilant companions who were cavorting on snowbanks or grazing glacier lilies.
When the hunter materialized within striking range, the ten-pound rodents vanished as
if swallowed by the mountain. After a brief investigation, the wolverine scaled an escarpment as steep as a cow's face. Faster than seemed possible, he was out of sight.

As I watched this drama unfold, a swarm of lady bugs swirled around me. Some
crawled on my legs and arms. One nipped my neck as if mistaking the green parka-clad

The billy goat I watched beneath the Heavenly Twins as a wolverine hunted marmots. (Photo by author)

intruder for an oversized aphid. Surveying all this from a wedge of granite encircled by pink-petaled heather and yellow-plumed groundsels was a lone billy goat. Like a benign ruler of a magic kingdom, maybe he, like me, regarded everything in perfect order on his mountain.

To me, the mountain goat is the alpine ecosystem's superstar, emblematic of the wildest of America's wildlands. Why goats sometimes display an irruptive nature and wandering tendencies when we've plopped them in a new home is unclear to those who study such things. This nature demonstrates ecological plasticity in the species—far more innate flexibility than we see in most native populations that have been anchored on the same piles of rocks for hundreds of generations. Although we still have much to learn about this enigmatic beast of the peaks, its paradoxical behavior offers hope that the mountain goat will persevere despite the insults we inflict on its environment. But that's no excuse for indifference, insensitivity, or inaction. Only our benevolence and active stewardship can ensure that future generations of wide-eyed admirers may marvel at the American mountain goat's life on the rocks.

DOI: 10.5876_9781607322924.c009

Epilogue

Only by spending intense time can you know and develop real intimacy with a place. In so doing, you begin to discover features, relations, and worth that casual visitors seldom see. The place—whether a Midwest marsh or New England woodlot, coastal estuary or headland, prairie potholes or desert canyons—then becomes part of you and you part of it. This connection is the germ and nourishment of conservation passion, not merely half-hearted advocacy.

My time in the Bitterroots cut a deep swathe in my person. That wedge of the mountain goat's realm became a kindred domicile. Besides the grand features named on USGS maps, smaller folds and twists in the landscape earned their own names that lodged in my lexicon: Cave Canyon, Maybilly Cliffs, and Nixon's Nose became cousins of the grand peaks that geographers had coined Castle Crag, Sky Pilot, and the Heavenly Twins.

This familiarity fondly endures nearly four decades after closing my camp in Fred Burr Canyon. Since then, fires have swept timbered slopes, thickets have replaced abandoned beaver ponds only to be cropped by more beaver, and generations of goats have come and gone. Yet the mesmerizing complexity and spirit of the land lives on. A sign in the gym where I exercise reads, "If

Alone at the top of the world. (Photo by author)

you don't take care of your body, where will you live?" So too, we must nurture the mountain to nurture the mountain goat.

This is only to say that all life is a product of the land, something wildlife ecologist Aldo Leopold illustrated so eloquently in his writings a half century and more ago. The land, weather, and DNA have conspired in bearing a bounty of life so diverse that each year field biologists catalog "new" species, even as others become destined for the bone-yard of the extinct. Some varieties are so beguiling, so reminiscent of ourselves in form or behavior, or so awe-inspiring in the feats they perform, that in admiration we elevate them above others in our value system. In that respect the mountain goat does us double duty. It recreates us spiritually, but also serves as protector—if our conservation ethic prevails—of a tapestry of species that share its high-country home.

Over the millennia, natural selection—the maestro of how life forms have come to be—has orchestrated sinew and snow and gravity and grit into a masterpiece: a beast of rock in wool, our American mountain goat. Every facet of its being shouts that it wants just to live high and free and solitary. And it will, if we but let it.

One last look. (Photo by author)

DOI: 10.5876_9781607322924.c010

Acknowledgments

Although the seed remained dormant for many years, writing this book is something I'd always known I would do. That seed was the animal itself and the way time among them enriched my education and launched my career. My graduate studies so long ago were mentored by Bart O'Gara, Phil Wright, Bob Ream, and others. My time in the Selway-Bitterroot Wilderness Area firmly planted my boots and my heart in the science and the art of wildlife biology, helping me understand both the scope and importance of the occupation. But the nourishment for the writing came from the growing struggle the mountain goat and so many other species face in this human-dominated world.

Any book project is a collaborative effort, even if but one author's name appears on the cover. Several colleagues were kind enough to review drafts of the work. I thank Douglas Chadwick, Steeve Côté, Marco Festa-Bianchet, Gayle Joslin, Jim Peek, Mike Thompson, Erik Beever, and Andrew Smith for their advice and constructive comments. My thanks also to Laney Hicks for the drawings of mountain goats on pages 129 and 130, and to the other photographers who graciously donated the use of their images.

Although we met long after the years when I lived among mountain goats, my wife Diana knows better than anyone how important this project was to me. Her suggestions, patience, and love throughout the writing and editing process are invisibly stamped throughout the book.

I also thank the wildlife biologists and managers from western Canada and the United States who answered my questions, provided reports, publications, and discussion, and offered their encouragement with this project. I am grateful to my editor, Jessica d'Arbonne, that the University Press of Colorado took a chance on a project about a relatively unknown species and accorded the mountain goat and its conservation a larger following.

DOI: 10.5876_9781607322924.c011

Suggested Reading

To read the original research and learn more detail about the topics covered in this book, including biology, ecology, natural history, and conservation of the mountain goat, I suggest the following published references.

Beever, E. A., and J. Belant, editors. 2011. *Ecological Consequences of Climate Change: Mechanisms, Conservation, and Management.* CRC Press, Boca Raton, FL.

Brandborg, S. M. 1955. "Life History and Management of the Mountain Goat in Idaho." Idaho Wildlife Bulletin 2: 1–142.

Chadwick, D. H. 1983. *A Beast the Color of Winter: The Mountain Goat Observed.* Sierra Club Books, San Francisco.

Côté, S. D., and M. Festa-Bianchet. 2003. "Mountain Goat, *Oreamnos americanus.*" In *Wild Mammals of North America: Biology, Management, and Conservation*, edited by G. A. Feldhammer, B. Thompson, and J. Chapman, 1061–75. Johns Hopkins University Press, Baltimore, MD.

Côté, S. D., S. Hamel, A. St-Louis, and J. Mainguy. 2013. "Do Mountain Goats Habituate to Helicopter Disturbance?" *Journal of Wildlife Management* 77(6):1244–1248.

Festa-Bianchet, M., and S. D. Côté. 2008. *Mountain Goats: Ecology, Behavior, and Conservation of an Alpine Ungulate.* Island Press, Washington, DC.

Gonzalez-Voyer, A., K. G. Smith, and M. Festa-Bianchet. 2003. "Dynamics of Hunted and Unhunted Mountain Goat Populations." *Wildlife Biology* 9: 213–18.

Houston, D. B., E. G. Schreiner, and B. B. Moorhead. 1994. *Mountain Goats in Olympic National Park: Biology and Management of an Introduced Species.* US National Park Service Scientific Monograph NPS/NROLYM/NRSM–94/25. National Park Service, Port Angeles, WA.

Intergovernmental Panel on Climate Change. 2007. Climate Change 2007: Synthesis Report; Contribution of Working Groups I, II and III to the Fourth Assessment Report of the Intergovernmental Panel on Climate Change. Core Writing Team, R. K. Pachauri and A. Reisinger, editors. IPCC, Geneva, Switzerland.

Joslin, G. 1988. "Life on the Edge." *Montana Outdoors* 19(3): 2–7.

Mountain Goat Management Team. 2010. "Management Plan for the Mountain Goat (*Oreamnos americanus*) in British Columbia." British Columbia Management Plan Series, Ministry of Environment, Victoria.

Nowak, R. M. 1999. *Walker's Mammals of the World*, vol. 2. Johns Hopkins University Press, Baltimore, MD.

Rice, C. G., and D. Gay. 2010. "Effects of Mountain Goat Harvest on Historic and Contemporary Populations." *Northwestern Naturalist* 91: 40–57.

Smith, B. L. 1988. "Criteria for Determining Age and Sex of American Mountain Goats in the Field." *Journal of Mammalogy* 69(2): 395–402.

Toweill, D. E., S. Gordon, E. Jenkins, T. Kreeger, and D. McWhirter. 2004. "A Working Hypothesis for Management of Mountain Goats." In *Fourteenth Biennial Symposium of the Northern Wild Sheep and Goat Council*, edited by W. Heimer, D. Toweill, and K. Hurley, 5–45. Wyoming Game and Fish Department, Cody, WY.

White, K. S., G. W. Pendleton, D. Crowley, H. J. Griese, K. J. Hundertmark, T. McDonough, L. Nichols, M. Robus, C. A. Smith, and J. W. Schoen. 2011. "Effects of Sex, Age, and Climate on Mountain Goat Survival in Coastal Alaska." *Journal of Wildlife Management* 75(8): 1731–44.

Wilson, D. E., and D. M. Reeder, editors. 2005. *Mammal Species of the World: A Taxonomic and Geographic Reference*, 3rd edition. Johns Hopkins University Press, Baltimore, MD.

Also by Bruce L. Smith

*Imperfect Pasture: A Century of Change at the
National Elk Refuge in Jackson Hole, Wyoming*

*Wildlife on the Wind: A Field Biologist's Journey
and an Indian Reservation's Renewal*

*Where Elk Roam: Conservation and Biopolitics
of Our National Elk Herd*